Damaged Goods

A True Story

of

Adoption

Music

People & Choices

For my two girls,

Lily and Katya

With love x

First Published in March 2011

This Reformatted Edition was published in July 2011 under ISBN 1463691513 and 9781463691516

Copyright © 2011 by Julian Wolfendale.

The moral right of the author has been asserted.

All rights reserved

No part of this document may be reproduced or transmitted in any form or by any means, electronic, mechanical, photocopying, recording, or otherwise, without prior written permission of Julian Wolfendale.

All photo's used are either the property of the author, or used with the owner's permission and may not be used or reproduced in any way.

Suffolk Libraries		
AmAZ		12/15
362.734		

This is my story. The people, places and events are real, though I have changed some names. No offence is meant to anyone else that I have mentioned, who think they might recognise themselves, or indeed to anyone that I have omitted, including my faithful old dog,Grolsch, who came to many gigs and parties with me, life's too damn short.

My thanks go to:

Amanda, for her love, inspiration and help, in sorting out both myself and the contents of this book.

All my Families, the Wolfendales, the Showlers, the Copemans and the Browns.

My oldest friend Jam, Douggie, Mr Moore, Hann & Matt, Francis, Paul the Photographer, Mr T, Steve Spon, The Village boys and girls and Mad Dave Barr.

Lt. Colonel A.J. Chadwick and Greasy Fletch, the best teachers anyone ever had.

Mr Cas Billy and Mr Michael Clarke, the best managers anyone ever had, who stood by me whilst all around me fell, and of course, to all those others who made this story.

Those that did not make it this far, you are missed.

J x

Damaged Goods

A True Story

of

Adoption

Music

People & Choices

Music is like life. As we only have so many days, so there are only so many notes. People put them together to make sense from all the chaos. The mental landscapes created by listeners, are as numerous as all the notes, in all the music ever written. They are both fleeting and immortal, imagined and yet as real and bright as anything in creation. When words are added, your imagination puts you into the tale woven by the lyrics.

Like reading a good book, laying in bed at night in the dark listening to your favourite music, takes you to another world, where you can find stories, emotions and memories from other people's lives. We twist them around until they fit our own, allowing us to live out our dreams and desires, through someone else's and giving vent to our hidden feelings and emotions. From sweeping sagas of love and loss, to adrenaline filled snapshots of youth, stories of the road and endless other possible lives, they're all there.

People and music are inseparable and songs are like our children, well, good ones anyway - they start out small and grow bigger and they have our dreams in them.

Knowing that someone else has felt the way that you do is part of the magic. It stops you from feeling alone. Sometimes it can seem that a song was written just for you, by someone you never met, because our stories are often not that different - we all live out our lives in the same world.

This isn't a music book, it's a story of sorts, but for me, music has always been part of my life, so it is intertwined with the words of this book.

Damaged Goods

I was born at the beginning of the sixties and grew up through them, the seventies, the eighties and nineties. I had an older brother and two younger sisters, all adopted, and we all lived together in a big house, set back from the road down a gated driveway at the top of a village, which was situated between two towns, surrounded by woods.

The house I grew up in.

Its big garden looked out over the valley and you could see for miles. It was before the new city of Milton Keynes was built and there were still brickworks in one of the towns in those days. The smoke from its chimneys often mixed with the clouds to give wonderful psychedelic sunsets, which I used to sit and stare at for hours, seeing imaginary coastlines and islands that I used to dream of running off to.

It was a time when there was still a music business, rather than it being the business of music, as it has become today. It was a magical time and place, when Top of the Pops and radio 1 still ruled the waves, and the world was without mobile phones and computers.

Phones still had bells in then and we used to race through the house to answer it before our parents. If you wanted to speak to someone, you had to arrange a day and time and wait for it to ring, either that or write them a letter and wait for the reply.

Not that I was ever up, but TV finished at midnight with the national anthem, followed by a blank screen. We didn't even have a TV in our house until I was 7 and that was a little black and white portable.

Apart from watching the kids stuff, like Vision On, Hector's House and Mr Ben, Belle & Sebastian and Captain Scarlet, I learned, to my surprise, the difference between a guerrilla and a gorilla, watching all the news stories on the war in Vietnam and hid behind the sofa when the theme tune to Doctor Who came on.

I remember going to a music workshop that had been organised for a week at Cleo Laine's house, in the next village, which was hosted by Rolf Harris. He was amazing, showing us how to make music with all sorts of household things and I met a boy called Storky there, who was a year older than me and already very good at music. I wasn't to see him again for another 15 years, but it was a great week and a lot of fun.

In the music that was around at the time, there was Medicine Head singing 'One and One is One' and The New Seekers were teaching the world to sing, with promises of everlasting summers and staying young forever, but there was always a shadow to be found too, like an evil twin, from 'Honey' by Bobby Goldsboro to Terry Jacks' dark 'Seasons in The Sun.' It was life's reality check, reflected in song.

Damaged Goods

From the Charleston and New Orleans Jazz of the twenties, through the rock and roll and Calypso of the 50's, r & b and beat/hippie folk of the 60's and the rock, glam, disco and punk of the 70's, to the mix of all of those that is around today, there's always been an undercurrent, like an engine revving for a burnout, forever waiting for the green light, like I was.

Keep it there. That's what it's for.

Every month seemed to bring new shows from America, Tomorrow's World heralded weekly new inventions for a bright future, always just around the corner, in a world in the final stages of recovery from two world wars. Adverts sold the idea of beauty and success and everything was go, go, go.

Both us and the world were young, with our whole life still stretching out in front of us. The pace of it all was such a buzz. But for me, at that age, the most important thing was Top of the Pops and Radio 1/247mw. Thursdays at 20 past 7. It was the only music show on TV and I lived for it! The theme tune was the CCS instrumental cover of Led Zeppelin's 'Whole Lotta Love' and those power chords grabbed me every week.

There would follow across the screen a parade, of the brightest, shiniest people of the moment, all looking like they were having a damn good time. I'm sure everyone has their memories of that show, the bands and singers that made them sit up and look harder. Sweet, Roxy Music, T.Rex, Mott the Hoople, Cockney Rebel and all the other Glam Rockers were regular visitors to my childhood sitting room. Leo Sayer coming on in full Pierrot outfit and singing the wonderful 'I won't let the show go on,' Bowie wearing tights and make up and David Essex dressed like a gypsy, singing the weird 'Rock On.'

All the bands from America seemed like the real gods to me though - The Commodores, The Stylistics and Earth Wind and Fire - all glitter, waistbands and big hair. Disco was all over it too, Tina Charles, Baccara, The Village People, even the lovely Pan's People. Damn, how could I get an invite to the party that all of them seemed to be living in? Bit of a job at eight years old...

Once a year, there was the Eurovision Song Contest too. I remember seeing and falling in love with Clodagh Rogers and both of the girls from Abba. Whilst on TV there was Dora from Follyfoot, Jenny Hanley from Magpie, Aqua Marina from Stingray and all the other beautiful women who drifted across the screen in the movies, from Rita Hayworth and Sophia Loren to Jane Seymour and the very lovely Caroline Munro.

Damaged Goods

I was looking forward, from the word go. I didn't have a clear idea of where I was looking, just somewhere else – somewhere better. It had to exist.

I listened to the words of the songs that I heard, and soaked up all the stories I saw on the TV.

Families were nice to each other on The Waltons and Little House on the Prairie. People in love kissed each other and talked and laughed. It didn't seem like that at home though and I just wanted to get away. But it was all I knew. All I had. If someone had asked me what I wanted to do with my life back then, that's what I would have said.

I could start right back at the beginning, but any day will do really, from my memories from when I was very young, from chasing my brother around the Tower of Pisa in Italy when I was 4, to riding a donkey on the beach in Spain when I was 6, or sitting in little boats to get to Elba and Corfu. We used to get taken abroad on holiday with Mum and Dad a lot when we were tiny, though this changed to camping in England and France when we were older and there were six of us.

This isn't an Enid Blyton book, or an A.A. Milne rhyme though.

16

When we were little I shared a bedroom with my adopted brother. He was 11 months older than me and seemed to wake up angry every day, looking for a fight.

At the age of 8 his choice of opponents was limited in that house. I was bigger than him, but I just wanted to be left alone. It was kind of ok really though, I knew that older brothers are supposed to be horrible when you're little. I wasn't crazy but sometimes when we'd fight, over anything, I'd let him punch himself out, but sometimes though, something would click in my head and I'd stop and look at him. A deep throated laugh would come from somewhere inside of me as he hit me and I'd just stare at him. He'd stop then, suddenly unsure and look at me. He knew then that he wouldn't win that time, and say I was crazy and back off. Maybe he was right.

At night, if he wanted something, he often couldn't be bothered to get up, so woke me and threatened me, until I went and got it for him. The thing about it I didn't like the most though, was that I still thought there was something lurking in the shadows, by the front door, at night time and maybe there was.

That old house had a real bad atmosphere, I knew that much. The previous owners, who had built it, told Mum and Dad that the land it was built on was haunted and that the parquet flooring that covered the whole of downstairs, was the remains of the World War Two battleship, HMS Hood.

Anyway, the last thing I wanted was a fight at that time of night. I was more worried about surviving everything else that went on.

I used to imagine my real parents turning up one day and whisking me off in their arms to safety, but it never happened of course.

If someone had told me that the world of TV, film and music was all pretend, that there weren't any real people like that out there, I don't know what I'd have done. Music saved my life. I decided that I wasn't going to grow up like

17

my family. It wasn't like I was made in their mould. I'd grow up good in spite of my beginnings.

These were my waking dreams though. For a future I couldn't see. My sleep didn't go so well. It was filled with nightmares, night after night, often the same one, over and over. Terrified wasn't a good way to start the day, but it wasn't like I wasn't used to it, it keeps you on your guard. I even made this cardboard box thing, with a cut out for my neck and kisses painted inside in red, which I'd put over my head and sing Elvis love songs to myself, until I felt better. I felt safe in there, for a while, my own little world, until after a few months, my brother trod on it and it was thrown away. I was good at surviving and recovering though. This was normal. Life went on.

Me and my brother.

At weekends I'd go to my friend Jam's house, my best friend since playschool, which his mum used to run. I could watch ITV there, with High Chaparral and Westerns and war films. His mum and dad weren't like mine. We'd spend the sunny days out in the fields and woods. They became the Wild West, or battlefields. We'd build camps, crawl along hedges and rows of corn like commando's, with our sheath knives and airguns.

If it was raining, his bedroom would become the deck of a warship, or a saloon in a John Wayne movie. We lived a hundred heroic lifetimes and saved a hundred damsels in distress together, even cutting our hands once, to become blood brothers, when we were playing Red Indians.

We'd go down to the rec,' where his dad played cricket on Saturdays. We'd watch for a bit, then sneak around the edge of the field and creep into his land rover, where we always found a bag of boiled sweets under the dashboard. We thought he never knew, but there was a new bag there every week. Bless him.

Me aged 5.

Damaged Goods

On schooldays, I'd go down to our Nanny's house for tea sometimes after school, until mum got back from work at the hospital. She was a doctor. I never wanted her to come and get me and never wanted to leave when she did.

The other thing was that my parents only listened to classical music. That was in the sitting room, where we weren't allowed in without knocking. Usually it was just dad in there, sitting in his armchair listening, with only the glow of the log fire for company.

Sometimes I'd be allowed to stay, laying on the rug staring in to the embers, hypnotised by the flames. They'd play us Prokofiev's Peter and the Wolf, narrated by Sean Connery sometimes and think that was our idea of fun. I liked his voice but the music just didn't do it for me. The only non classical record in the house was an old Joan Baez bluegrass Lp, left by a nephew who had visited. I loved that record. It was different. I got Dad to play it whenever I could. I still have it now and still love the sound of banjos.

There used to be an old acoustic guitar that sat high up on a shelf, gathering dust, which I used to stare at and dream of being a pop star, which Dad must have noticed. He knew someone in the village who played and one day surprised me, by arranging some lessons.

The guy was Spanish and once a week I'd go down to his house, where he taught me how to play, sitting in his front room or out on the front step, looking out over the valley. I lapped it up and was getting quite good, when one day Dad told me he had gone. I didn't quite understand why, as his wife was still there, but that was the end of my lessons. I'd learnt the basics though and I have loved guitars, as well as Spanish music, ever since.

Our Nanny's house was different. Her husband Derek was always going off shooting in the fields, tinkering with his old cars or sitting in the front room, cleaning and oiling his guns. Sometimes he used to let me hold them and pull the triggers, before he locked them away. They had a big Alsatian dog called Rusty too, that we all used to play with, even my baby sister, he was great.

Cars weren't like they are today, nor were MOT's as strict. The roads were full of rusting, multicoloured vehicles, with different coloured wings and bonnets and weekends saw most people tinkering with them, just to keep them running.

Every week my Nanny would go down to John Menzie's in town and buy a new 45rpm. Pop music! I'd sit and listen, rapt by the sound. She played Lynn Anderson singing 'Rose Garden' all the time and I wanted to get lost in the magical world she sang about. I guess that's what I did when I was older, but for now, it was at least a temporary escape.

Only whilst I was awake though – every night was haunted by bad dreams. Sometimes I'd have one that seemed like someone else's, to start with anyway, almost like it was tricking me into dreaming it, just to scare me all the more. Sometimes the line between my nightmares and my waking life became real thin. Here's one, that often started out differently but always ended at the same place;

I'm walking down a sunlit path in the woods, not a care in the world. Music suddenly starts up, something from Holst's Planet Suite – 'Mars the Bringer of War' I think. Somewhere far off I hear a rumbling like distant thunder and I know it's going to grow into a rhythm. It does. Oh shit. I try and ignore it, I can't remember why but I really don't want to hear it. The trees get closer together and the sky gets darker, leaves whirl in the wind leaving skeletal trunks with branches like claws, waving in the storm. It looks like winter.

I'm not lost but I know I shouldn't be here. This isn't my woods. I'm getting scared. The wind sighs and howls and rain comes down in sheets around me. The path gets thinner and a feeling of unease hangs in dark puddles on the ground. Just then I see a light in the distance but it's not the kind of light that saves you, it's the kind that lies to you. I've seen it before and I know where it's taking me now. I really don't want to go.

The music fades and the sound gets louder until I can feel it all over me and I hear myself begin to howl, like a dog.

Damaged Goods

Then the path ends and I see my destination. It's a small brick built barn, with two floors, the light just a metal cover with a bare bulb beneath it, outside the upper window, above the door. That window, I know that window – it's metal framed single glazed, the small cracked panes are black and stare back at me with dead fish eyes, like the ones at home.

Now I know what that sound is. I did all along. It's like a steam hammer, shaking me and the building - even the ground seems to move. I really don't want to go in there, but it draws me on. There's no one going to help me. The only person there is, is the one waiting for me inside and I know who it is, I always did. The door opens. I scream and wake up breathless, sitting bolt upright, the sweat pouring off me in the dark. There's no one here to help me either. My brother swears and throws a book at me.

So was that real or is this? I don't know and it takes a while to fade, as I lay waiting for the dawn to chase it away.

Another one was I'd be somewhere in the house, standing in the hallway or sitting at the table for supper, with Mum and Dad sat next to me, talking to each other. Suddenly, I'd notice a hole opening up in the floor and I'd start screaming. They didn't seem to hear me as the hole got bigger and bigger until I could see a wrinkled, white haired old witch coming out. She'd grab me with her claw like hands and shaking me, drag me back down into the hole with her and though I'd be screaming and screaming, Mum and Dad wouldn't even notice. I'd still be screaming when I woke up from that one too.

Another was I had been left alone in Mum's mini traveller at the top of the lane by my Nannies' house, when the car started rolling down the hill. I was laughing until I tried to pull the handbrake on harder, like I'd seen my mum do, but it didn't work. The lane seemed to be longer than in real life and I just kept rolling, faster and faster, the whole car shaking as it careered down the lane, until I woke up, just before hitting the trees.

I did sometimes have nice dreams though. I had one where the Osmonds came to our house for tea once, all of them filing in through the front door, with me worrying about how to keep their visit secret.

Whether they were good or not, my dreams always seemed to hang around for the rest of the day and I was often, for a few hours, worried and unsure as to whether or not they had been real. I know that sometimes I wished they were.

Me and my designer play clothes!

Damaged Goods

Down the bottom of the hill, by the village pub, there was an old beamed barn that had been converted into a house. It was next to a big, walled lodge house that had been owned by the Kray Twins until they got put away.

Apparently, they used to arrive on a Friday night, with a few friends, in big black cars and go over to the pub. They were friendly and courteous to everyone in there and usually insisted on buying everyone's drinks all night. At closing time, they would invite everyone over the road to their house and take them down to the cellar, which had been converted into a casino of sorts. There were green baize tables with a walnut bar at the end, with every kind of spirit you could imagine, all free.

They were some raucous, late nights down there, but without a hint of trouble, ever. There was no real TV or press coverage out in the sticks in those days and it came as a shock to everyone, when they were arrested and put in gaol. Everyone said they had seemed like such gentlemen.

My Nanny's husband Derek was a lorry driver, who used to frequent the pub in those days and he spent a few wild nights with them. After the case was over, he suddenly clammed up whenever I asked about them. I couldn't understand it, they sounded like fun to me. He had told me a tale of setting out to walk back from town, early one summer's morning, after being dropped off after a delivery to Wales.

As he passed the fence around the scrap dealers yard, he heard what he thought was a radio that had been left on, blaring music. He had climbed up to peer over the fence to see what it was and saw a full orchestra, in dinner suits, playing to a big party in there. Amongst other dapper looking people, the Krays stood there smiling and, recognising him from the pub, invited him in. He didn't go though, as he had to get home, so thanked them, apologising and carried on walking.

It was the scrap dealer who took over the running of the house after that. He decided that he wanted the converted barn too and tried to buy it from the strange looking couple

24

of men who lived there. One of them had a bleached blond bob, wore what looked like makeup and ladies sunglasses to me and carried a handbag. People whispered things about him but he was always polite when I said hello and seemed very kind.

I guess he looked like an easy target, but he wasn't. He got his legs broken when he wouldn't sell, but even then took the criminals to court. Just because he wasn't butch and looked different didn't mean he was scared. I remember being very impressed with that. My parents didn't want to talk about it either though, I couldn't understand why not. Probably the same reason that they didn't let us watch ITV on the tele, whatever that was.

I never could see the reasoning with that really, as Dad was quite happy for me to sit up late on Saturdays and watch the late night double horror bill on BBC2. Those old Hammer films might have been a bit dated, but I hadn't seen any modern ones and they were creepy enough, especially sitting on your own in the dark at that age.

There were werewolves, vampires and various mad professors, with Lon Chaney, Boris Karloff, Bela Lugosi, Christopher Lee and Peter Cushing, all hamming it up for all they were worth. Of course, they also had all those lovely Hammer girls, like Ingrid Pitt, Ursula Andress and Raquel Welch, in various states of undress, which made them even better.

It was around then that I sneaked into the old town cinema and sat puffing away on cigarettes with a few others, watching the smoke swirl in the light of the projector as we watched the new film out, 'The Exorcist.' It wasn't like the old horror films at all and I thought it was really, properly scary, with the music being just as bad as the film.

Dad took me, my brother and Jam and his brother to see the new James Bond film, Live and Let Die, there around the same time and I don't know which I enjoyed more really.

Damaged Goods

A year or two later he took us all to see the Slade film 'Flame' and that was another shocker, not at all the happy glamfest we'd expected. It was good though, tough, gritty and grownup and it had some great songs in it.

Dad had always read to us at bedtime and I think he enjoyed the books we discovered as much as we did. My favourites were The Hobbit and Lord of The Rings which were great books to drift off to sleep to.

When I started reading to myself, an Australian book called Bottersnikes and Gumbles was the one I read the most, until Stig of The Dump came out, which I read to myself, four times in a row. I started taking books from Dad's bookcase to read too, from Jock of the Bushveldt to some of his Science Fiction. I even read some of his poetry books, like Shelley and Keats, which I liked, but found a bit hard going to be honest.

Then I read Frankenstein. Under the bedclothes at night, with the wind blowing outside, that was a great book and I soon graduated to the ghost stories of M.R. James, some of which were shown as films on the TV at Christmas time and were very creepy.

Though full of atmosphere, dread and suspense, they lacked real gore and violence and I found that in the Pulp Western novels of J.T. Edson about the cowboy, Edge.

My love of horror, western and crime books, as well as any other dark stories has stayed with me and I still love a good shocker, as well as the wonderful American Noir crime books of James Ellroy.

Whenever it was dark and we were driving home, I used to curl up on the floor, in the back of my mum's car, listening to the noise of the exhaust. I felt safe and warm down there. I remember getting home from somewhere one night and looking up and seeing the stars. I'd never really noticed them before. I stood there staring for ages. Out in the sticks there were hardly any street lights in those days and what few there were, all went off at midnight.

But that night it was dark and clear and I saw a thousand twinkling lights looking down at me. It made everything else seem small and unimportant then, even me and my life, which was kind of comforting.

Some days I would sit alone in the garden and just stare. I'd stare out at the hedge, the trees and the view. I found that with practice, if I stared at something for long enough, without even slightly moving my eyes or blinking, a haze would begin to appear around whatever object I was concentrating on, like a halo. Eventually, after about ten minutes, everything else in the background would go dark around it and then alternate, like someone flicking between a negative and a positive image. If I really kept going, even the object itself would disappear, leaving only dark swirling shades of purple before my eyes, I always loved seeing colours. One tiny flick of my eyes would clear it, but I'd usually carry on for an hour or more, feeling like I'd been transported into outer space, the way they did on Star Trek.

Damaged Goods

Sometimes, my Nanny's daughter, Auntie Pauline and her boyfriend, Mr. Steve, would baby sit for us. They were about ten years older than me and were always trying to get me and my brother to go to bed early. I couldn't understand why at that age and used to want to stay up with them and watch whatever film was on, whilst my brother of course wanted to watch the football, but we used to go to bed eventually.

Sometimes, Auntie Pauline and Mr. Steve would take us out at weekends too. They used to take us to the stock car racing at the nearby racetrack. It was brilliant, sort of like being in an Elvis film. We used to get coca cola and hotdogs and stuff and always came home with loads of stickers for STP and all sorts of oils and tyres. Eventually though, it came to a stop one Saturday.

We were in the stands when two cars crashed into each other and a wheel came flying up over the fence, hitting a lady in the head and killing her right in front of us. Although there seemed to be lots of screaming and shouting I didn't feel traumatised, I thought it was exciting. In any case, the race was stopped and we all had to go home early. Sadly I never went again. I guess my parents didn't approve. Shame, I loved the smell of the oil and petrol, the sound of the crowd and watching all those cars burning around the track, I thought it was like America. There were other kinds of fun to be had though.

The next weekend there was a gymkhana up at their friend's farm. A big marquee had been put up in the field next to the farmhouse, with a bar and a disco. By the time we got there, all the eventing had finished and the disco was playing loud music, with everyone drinking, dancing and shouting. It seemed to me like the whole village had turned up.

The next thing I knew was that Mr. Steve, Uncle Malc and even Auntie Pauline were all fighting. Not with each other though, there was an enormous brawl going on. I thought it was great, like something from a Western! Someone got thrown over the disco and the music stopped and all of a sudden it seemed like everyone was joining in, punches and kicks everywhere.

I sat at the back and watched for ages, it seemed to go on forever, until at last, a little panda car turned up with a policeman in it. He got out and started to shout at everyone, until their friend Dave landed a punch on him and knocked him over, his helmet falling off and then proceeded to pour a pint on his head.

I laughed and laughed, I thought this was great! The grownups didn't seem to think so though, everyone seemed to have black eyes, cuts and bleeding noses and Mr. Steve, my Uncle Malc and Dave managed to scarper off home in a friends Jag, just as more police turned up. A few others weren't so lucky and were carted off to the A&E dept. then the police station, to 'calm down a bit,' or so I was told. Excellent weekend!

The following week, I was down at my Nanny's house for tea, after school. We had just sat down to eat when we heard someone shouting, out by the front gate. My Nanny went out to see what all the fuss was about and came back in looking distinctly unimpressed. She said to my Uncle Malc that his friend Dave, from the farm, was outside, drunk again and wanting another fight. Great! Malc told her to tell him that he was eating his tea and would come and fight him afterwards.

He sat there and polished off his meal, pulled his work boots back on and went outside. I peered up over the bottom of the window and watched them go at it on the drive. Blimey, they were fierce! Eventually though, his friend had enough and got up from the road and staggered off back up to the farm, swearing and limping. Malc came back in with a cut eye and bleeding nose and just said 'right, that's that then, where's me pudding?,' then went off into the front room, to practice his dancing.

Apparently a week or so later, when he had recovered enough to go out, Dave asked Uncle Malc to say that he'd been kicked by a horse, to save his embarrassment. I loved being with that family, life was exciting and unpredictable,

29

Damaged Goods

every minute lived to the full. I wanted to live with them and stay there forever.

The same summer, I was with my mum, on the way to the hospital where she worked. It was a Saturday morning and I had arranged to meet my friend Dave down the rec' in the afternoon. There were these new toffee lollipops in the village shop and I had given him my pocket money to get me one. We stopped off at the petrol station that she and dad had an account at in town. I liked going there as they had a big Alsatian dog, like my Nannies.

Mum went in to pay and the dog padded across the forecourt to see me. I had stroked him hundreds of times, but this time, whether it was the heat of the day, or that some lads had wound him up, banging on the window the night before, I don't know. I reached out to stroke him and he jumped up and bit me, sinking his fangs into my face. He gripped my cheek and jaw and growled. One of his claws went in my arm. I screamed like never before and I think it was that that made him let go.

My mum came running out, shouting at the dog and grabbed me, holding me against her as it ran off. My blood poured all over her white jumper and she just kept saying it was alright, over and over. It was strange, but it didn't hurt that much, once the initial shock wore off. An ambulance appeared and I was ok until I got in and saw my reflection in the green glass of the windows. My cheek was flapping open and I could see my teeth. I started crying again, out of fear I think, I didn't know what to do. All I could think about was that I wasn't going to get my sodding lollipop.

When I got to the hospital, my mum knew the plastic surgeon that worked there and got him to sew me up. I had a local anaesthetic and had seven little stitches in my face and two in my arm. I remember watching the gold thread go in and come out black. To be honest I kind of liked all the attention, especially from the nurses, who were very nice to me. Probably not the best way to get it though. I went home looking, I thought, very butch and now I had a scar like all the baddies in the films. Cool.

My brother was clever enough to get interested in things outside of the village, like football and fishing and was always off somewhere with his mates. He got in the local paper for being in the angling junior national and was also football mad and good at it, becoming an F.A. coach when he was older, teaching it at universities in America. He'd always want to watch it on the TV, even the results and we'd always argue about who was going to watch what, which usually ended in a fight. That kind of put me off sport really.

I thought I should find something that I did like, for myself, so I joined the local swimming club, which used to be held at the indoor pool at Stockgrove, before there was anywhere else nearby. I started to cycle the two miles there, every Wednesday evening and I started getting fit. I loved it. I seemed to be better at swimming under the water instead of on top of it though. I could swim 2 lengths under water and sit on the bottom and hold my breath for 4 minutes. That used to worry Stella, the lady who taught us, but it was great down there, like another world really. I got all my badges, including the mile swim and just when I was getting really good, the new leisure centre opened up in town a few miles away and the club moved premises. It was just too far for me to cycle and so I stopped going. I was upset to leave, but have always loved swimming ever since and I am still better underwater.

Damaged Goods

In the summer holidays, the thing I looked forward to the most was to go camping in the fields down behind the rec' with the rest of the gang. It was great. They did it every summer. We had our tents in a ring with a big bonfire in the middle and music blaring out from a radio.

There was a dairy in the village in those days, where lorries were loaded at night and left there for the early morning deliveries. Asking for trouble really. Just after dark, we'd set off for a raid. We tried to look innocent walking along the road to the other end of the village. Once we got near we climbed over the wall and crawled across the field on our stomachs, stopping when we heard a door slam, a dog bark or saw a light go on. Like commandos we froze in place and waited, without making a sound.

Once it was all quiet again we were off. The lorry shutters were never locked and we rolled them up, inch by inch, all the while holding our breath and looking around for a sign of movement. Bottles of 'Corona' and 'Farmer's Wife' fizzy drinks, milk, bread and even orange juice, were passed down from hand to hand, until we had enough. Then we closed the lorries quietly back up. 'Go, go!' we hissed to each other and this time ran across the field as fast as we could with our loot, expecting someone to come after us at any minute. When we got to the edge of the field, we were over the wall and down the road into the darkness. Made it!

Back at the campsite, it was cigarettes and bottles all round and we went over every detail of our mission, our success usually toasted by the older boys spraying us with lemonade, like racing drivers. The radio was tuned into an oldies show and was playing Pickettywitch's 'Same Old Feeling' and Mary Hopkin, singing 'Those were the days.' Surely it wasn't that long ago and I wondered if they ever really were the days, as this seemed pretty good to me. That was about the worst we got up to though, it was just fun really, no one got hurt.

I think the only person to get in trouble was a boy whose Mum wouldn't let him come camping. He left her a note saying that he'd gone fishing early in the morning and sneaked down to the campsite with his sleeping bag, after midnight. The older boys made me take his bag up to his mum's house the next morning, under threat of a hiding, knock on the door and ask his mum if he would be coming camping again that night. I heard her shouting up at him as I ran off back to the fields. Not very nice really, but they thought it was funny.

Summer went on and on and soon it was going to be my birthday. I always had good birthday bashes, the year before Mum had taken me and Jam and our two brothers to London, to see the Jesus Christ Superstar musical. It was so cool and not like the classical concerts they often dragged us to at all, with the singer playing Judas having a real good rock voice and we got to have a meal in a restaurant, next to the theatre afterwards. I did used to enjoy some of the operas and ballets they took us to sometimes though, the small stages and glittering costumes shining like a distant dream in the darkened theatres.

When my mum asked me what I wanted that year, I said I wanted a disco, instead of a party or outing. I had loads of 'Top of The Pops' and 'Hot Hits' albums, with all the latest stuff and I wanted to know what it felt like at a disco. My mum sent out the invitations and during the next week, we had loads of worried parents ringing up, asking exactly what would be going on. I was nine, what did they think - That we'd all be smooching with satin clad women and drinking scotch like Roger Moore? I wish.

It was a lovely hot day and we had all the patio doors open, with my music blaring out of dad's Phillips Hi-fi, which he wouldn't have appreciated if he'd been there. We all danced and danced outside on the patio, with Sweet, Slade, Pilot, The Rubettes, Billie Jo Spears and Scott Mackenzie singing 'San Francisco.' Mum and Dad had got me some new green high waister flares and an orange and white floppy collared shirt, to go with my spoon shoes and I felt very sharp. We even got my little sister dancing to Sweet's 'Hellraiser.'

Damaged Goods

It suddenly seemed a long time ago since I'd been decked out in Ladybird clothes and Clarks shoes.

We did stop and go in to play pass the parcel and stuff like that though and to have fizzy drinks and eat twiglets and crisps, which we only got at parties in those days. There was also my cake which mum had made, in the shape of a Winchester rifle like John Wayne's, which was very cool. It was a good party and we all managed to have a good time, with no babes or devil worshipping and with everyone going home safely.

We used to jump on any horse in the fields that we could get near enough to in those days and ride them bareback. We just hung onto their manes and went. We even tried it on a cow once, but only the once though, that was a painful mistake, getting bucked off and kicked.

I remember one time riding down the track to the farm where that Gymkhana had been, I slid around the horse's neck as it galloped along, hanging on for life as its hooves thundered in front of me. Scared me that did and that was when my Mum decided to get me some riding lessons with Ivan.

On my 10th Birthday she got Marilyn from the stables to come to our front door with a big white horse. She had blond hair, blue eyes and blue Jeans and was a real 70's babe. She led me all around the village for an hour or so and I felt like a king.

Not long after that the village disco started, it was for under 18's and held in the old parish hall. An old Teddy Boy from the village was the DJ and he always had all the latest releases. It was great, really. There were swirling disco lights and massive loud speakers. Soft drinks and crisps were sold in the little back room and after Top of The Pops, it became the thing that I most looked forward to. People came from all the surrounding villages and it was always packed with boys and girls.

The smell of over applied Brut, Old Spice and Charlie filled the air. They were the newest fragrances out and advertised all over the place. My Nanny started buying it for us at birthdays and Christmas and continued to do so until we were about 15, but everyone wore it back then. Ad's were great in those days and they used to advertise everything on the TV; Cigarettes, petrol, even milk and eggs! There were those annoying Charley Says safety adverts and even Les Gray from Mud used to do some, which were a whole lot more cheerful than the public information films, showing the dangers of playing near water and stuff, they should have been X rated!

All of us used to chuckle at the tagline for the Harmony hairspray one – 'Is she, or isn't she?' and there was the Nimble bread advert with the hot air balloon, which was about all that was in a slice of Nimble as I recall. Did anyone really eat that stuff?

We didn't have to as there was still an old village bakery then. The baker used to deliver our bread to the doorstep in the mornings, at which point, our Nanny would hide behind the door and blow raspberries, leaving us staring at him innocently. I remember her doing the same thing in Keymarkets and ducking behind an aisle, laughing herself silly.

Anyway, the Disco. All the boys would stand in line and do the old hands on belt loops rocker's dance, to Slade, Sweet and Nazareth, and we'd try and look like we knew how to dance to all the latest disco releases, like The Hues Corporation singing 'Rock The Boat' and Van McCoy doing 'The Hustle.' It was like finally, having our own nightclub.

35

Damaged Goods

The thing that we all looked forward to the most though, was the slow dances at the end. The last song of the night was always an instrumental of 'Who's Taking You Home Tonight,' by James Last and his Orchestra, but before that, we'd have already argued about which girl we were going to ask to dance, hoping that that pretty one we'd seen the week before would be there. We'd shuffle around the wooden floor, cuddling and kissing to The strains of Doctor Hook's 'A Little Bit More,' or The Commodores 'Three Times A Lady,' sometimes even putting a hand on their bum and feeling like film stars. I remember dancing with a quiet, pretty girl from our village a few times, a few years younger than me, whose name was Emma.

I also remember, sadly, finally having a fight outside over another girl, with my mate Jam. I immediately wished I hadn't, but the damage was done. Mates and girls don't mix, I learnt that that night. Shame. When he was older he fought for the British Karate Team, so I guess it's best to have those kind of falling outs when you're younger.

Sometimes when we were all hanging out in the rec,' the older boys would get bored and make us younger ones fight each other. They'd bet on who was going to win, then make us start. We weren't allowed any sticks or anything, but it was far from a game and if we didn't fight properly, they'd pick us up and throw us on top of the hawthorn hedge, which would cut you to ribbons.

Depending on who I was fighting, I'd sometimes stand there, trading punches for minutes on end, hoping my next one would be good enough to end it. Sometimes though I lost of course and it always hurt.

They weren't always such bullies though and sometimes they'd join in too, which was nice of them. We'd all have to play a game that they called Rollerbollock, after some violent film they'd been to see at the cinema. There were 2 teams, the ball was thrown in the air and whoever caught it had to get it to the opposite end of the rec.' Sounds simple enough but playing that game was the first time I got knocked out.

One of the older boys had the ball, a load of us jumped on him, and in the struggle that followed, he threw out a haymaker that landed squarely on my jaw. I was flat on my back seeing stars. When I didn't get up, he came over and said sorry and carried me over to the swings to recover. If I'm honest I guess I quite liked that game and the odd smack in the mouth never really hurt anyone, it was just one of those things.

Speaking of smacks in the mouth, there was a posh family who used to live in the vicarage, behind the rec.' They were very Seventies, all pretty and photogenic and called their parents by their first names, which I thought was very modern. We'd thrown loads of bangers over their fence before running and hiding in the fields, the November before and I don't think their Dad was very impressed with us lot. I was sort of going out with their daughter at school though, as little ones do.

She had one brother a couple of years older than me, who didn't normally mix with us as he went to Public school, but one day he did. The older boys were bored for a change and started picking on him. They kind of backed off when he stood up and offered them out though and I couldn't understand why, as he was younger than them. So I stood up and said that if no one else would fight him then I would, as I was sure it would be easy. Wrong, wrong, wrong!

They all giggled as I advanced and squared up to him, planning to kick him in the balls and end it quickly, but as I got within his range, he shot out a punch that landed right on my ear and stunned me. The rest were laughing out loud now so I couldn't stop, but every time I got near him, he dodged my punches and landed another perfect shot on my ear. It really started to hurt and after about 5 minutes I was getting a bit dazed, so I gave up. He said I was the bravest out of the lot of them and asked if any of the others wanted a go, which they all declined, unsurprisingly. I think they probably knew a bit more about him than I did.

Damaged Goods

The next week at school I asked his sister how he'd done it and she replied that he'd been doing boxing at school for 3 years. I was very impressed and wanted to learn how to do that. I did, later on, but I still have the lump on my left ear that he gave me to this day.

At school, the only things I ever got good reports for were English, Art and Running. Not sport, just running. I never liked team sports much, never felt the need to join in and see who was the best, but I could run all day long. The headmaster's words were 'Julian is surprisingly good at long distance running.' I think he was surprised that I was any good at anything actually. So was I.

Village school sports day, 1971. I'm second from the left!

My Art teacher was the only other person to write anything good about my work, though she did also say that all my pictures were of 'Rather sad subject matter.' As for the other subjects, I seemed to have had trouble concentrating for more than five minutes. I guess I was lazy, but whether I had trouble concentrating because I was lazy, or was lazy because I had trouble concentrating, I don't know. I didn't major in psychology.

We used to have organised runs across the fields behind the school and sometimes the dips in the fields were full of icy water, that was chest deep and we used to plunge into that without batting an eyelid. I loved it so much that I started to go running through the woods back in my village at the weekends too.

As for the rest of the sport though, I opted out and did needlework and cookery instead. The caretaker's wife used to teach cookery and we used to think it was hilarious to flick bits of dough up on the ceiling when she wasn't looking. By the end of term it looked like the roof of a cave, with all the dried dough hanging down like little stalactites.

The needlework was interesting too, I learned how to cut and sew all the different stitches, and also the class was all girls except for me, which made it even better – who wanted to be out playing football with the rest of the boys?

Another good thing about that school was that every day on the way to school, we had to drive past the Aston Martin factory. Ever since my mum had bought me the Ladybird book of cars, when I was six, I had loved cars and Aston Martins were very cool and posh, even Roger Moore had one, both in James Bond and The Persuaders, I knew even then that they cost as much as a house.

I used to drool at all the different models out on the forecourt as we drove past, but one day, parked outside the estate agents at the top of the school road as we went past, there was another strange looking sort of car. It was dark metallic blue and low to the ground and it looked more like a rocket ship to me.

Damaged Goods

I sneaked out of the school gate at playtime and ran up to it, gazing wondrously at the tan leather seats and all the dials and vents and things, trying to make out the top speed on the speedo-180mph! It even had a light on the centre armrest!

As I stood there, the owner came out and asked me if I liked it, telling me it was called a Lamborghini Espada. Now that was a name! When he got in and started it up, he gave me the thumbs up and revved the engine, before wheel spinning away up the road. Wow, that thing flew - what a noise, what a car! I decided that I liked Lamborghinis even more than the Astons after that.

One thing that was different in our house was Christmas. Every year, we were allowed into the sitting room on Christmas Eve, to choose and open one present from under the tree. On Christmas Day, we'd wake early and find our stockings at the end of the bed. That was the best bit really.

Dad was always miserable on Christmas Day, a family tradition of sorts.

We had to wait until 11o'clock to open the rest of our presents, as Dad had to go and pick up his mother and bring her up to the house. She was about 80 then, with white hair, always set perfectly, very elegant. She'd sit and have her glass of sherry in silence, whilst we all opened our presents. She'd always bring up a giant milky bar silver dollar for us, which was good.

After I was about 11, I'd sometimes go down to her little house for a cup of tea in the holidays. 'Want a cigarette boy?' she'd ask. She had smoked since she was little, when she used to live on a farm with her parents in Chertsey, which was then still a village, so it didn't bother her to see me smoke. My parents would have gone mad if they knew.

Sometimes, if she hadn't had too much sherry, she'd tell me stories of when she was young. She'd been a showgirl and a dancer in London. She had such tales, my eyes would be like saucers by the end. Like Tallulah Bankhead once turning up at an after show party with a shoebox full of Cocaine, which wasn't yet illegal in those days, you still got it in coca cola back then! I could almost hear the crowd and smell the greasepaint by the end.

Dad never spoke about her, I think he was embarrassed, but I thought it was great to have a gran who was cool like that, secretly. After she died, when I was about 19, I found an old photo portrait of her when she was young. She hadn't been kidding, she was beautiful.

The very best thing though was Boxing Day, when my godfather and his wife would come up to stay, from their home in London. They were great. My parents seemed to relax when they arrived and stayed that way for as long they stayed. He was the maths Master at Latimer school in London and also ran his old family hardware shop in Hanwell, from which he always bought me a calendar. The presents they bought us were out of this world, always just what a young boy wanted – miniature circular saws and drills that really worked, suits of armour from Hamley's, all sorts.

My godfather's nickname was The Admiral, in part due to his long white beard, but also as every year since I was a baby, we'd all go for a week's sailing on the Norfolk Broads and I'd always get to spend the week on their boat. It was mostly full of old wooden sailing boats in those days and they'd all look at cruisers with disdain, though I always thought they looked nice and roomy and comfortable.

Me sailing my godfather's boat on the Norfolk Broads 1974

The things I remember most about all those holidays are the smell of calor gas in the galley, the way the mist looked in the mornings, hanging across the water, all the funny little windmill shaped houses along the river at Potter Heigham and being scared silly, holding on for dear life as we tacked across Breydon Water in a storm, with the pots and pans flying across the bunks below decks and the boat tipping up at alarming angles in the gale. I did love sailing though.

When I was 12, the present they gave me is the only good thing I remember from that whole year – a skiing holiday in Nauders, near Innsbruck in Austria. Wow! It was him and two other teachers, and the sixth formers from the school. We flew out and arrived into the snow. Mum and Dad had bought me my skiing outfit and as soon as we arrived, we went and hired the Salomon ski's and got our lift passes.

It was perhaps unsurprising that I was looked upon as a kind of mascot by the all the older children. I think I made them laugh. They were all quite posh and here was this little 12 year old smoking and swearing with them. I thought the ski lifts were great and attacked all the different coloured pistes fearlessly within the first two days. Sitting at an outdoor cafe, at the top of a mountain, smoking Marlboro reds in the clear mountain air and drinking an ice cold lager, looking across the mountains I thought it was just brilliant. My godparents left me to my own devices for the most part, hanging out with all the teenagers.

One evening after another day's skiing, we were back in the room they all congregated in and I saw a girl and a boy French kissing. I thought it looked kind of horrible at first, but I kept watching. They seemed to enjoy it.

That night they took me along to the local disco with them all, which every self respecting European town had in the 70's. I was sat there in a little booth with a table, drinking a brandy and coke that I had found and feeling very grown up, when the older girl I had been watching earlier came and sat next to me. She told me she had seen me watching her kiss and asked what I thought. I was embarrassed and said I didn't really know and she said that she thought I was cute and asked if I wanted a go? Umm...yep! She was gentle with me. I remember she smelled like heaven and her mouth was the most amazing thing I had ever tasted. She told me she was 18. Damn I wanted to do that again! Lots.

We got up and had a dance to Candi Staton singing 'Young Hearts Run Free,' until her boyfriend came over and laughed at us and off she went. I kept dancing for the rest

Damaged Goods

of the night and I couldn't stop smiling. So this was what older people did at night. This was a great holiday!

Nauders, Austria 1976

A few nights later, my godfather took me out at 11 o'clock at night on a horse drawn sleigh ride, across the border in to Italy.

Snuggled up underneath some animal furs, we flew through the snow bound night for what seemed like hours. We arrived at a hotel in the middle of nowhere, just after midnight and sat in front of a massive roaring log fire, drinking hot Gluwien for ages.

The journey home was like being in Narnia. The sound of the horses and the rocking of the sleigh sending me to sleep as a thousand stars glittered across the white mountainscape. Wonderful.

On the very last night, the ski lift was opened up for anyone who wanted a last go down the mountain. We all went up and there were toboggans waiting for us. It wasn't dark, with the moon shining on the snow like a floodlight and we all set off together.

I can still see the trees rushing past us as we sped down to the bottom, the night split by screams and laughter. We had three or four goes all together, with no one getting hurt. I never wanted it to end, but it did – all too soon.

That year, the summer just kept getting hotter and hotter. It turned into a drought. The earth in the fields cracked like a desert and the crops all died, along with people's lawns and flowers. The smell of melting tarmac and creosoted fences was everywhere, there were adverts on the TV telling you how many inches of water to have in your bath, as showers were not yet common and it just stayed hot, hot, hot, 24 hours a day.

At the end of term, one of my friends invited me to stay for a week. He lived with his mum and dad, who were friends with mine, in a big old stone built house next to a forest. They were loaded. Big Mercedes, swimming pool, all that stuff. He had a treehouse in a giant oak tree at the edge of the woods that his dad had built, where we used to play. His dad smoked French cigarettes and cigars and kept them, along with his drink, in the cellar. Theirs was also the first place I had drunk orange juice, well, Haliborange anyway, as there were hardly any supermarkets then and nowhere really sold fruit juice, except sugary stuff in tins.

Sometimes, after watching Ron Ely playing Tarzan on the TV, we'd go and pinch a few cans and packets of cigarettes from the cellar and poke them up onto the ground outside, through the little bars in the cellar windows. We'd saunter innocently out through the house, then pick our stuff up and run across the field to the tree house as fast as we could, where we'd proceed to sit and smoke and drink.

We'd be out playing all day, damming up streams, throwing sticks at birds and stuff like that and we had sandwiches and crisps, so any smell would be gone by the time we returned.

It was his birthday party this week and they had put fairy lights all round the outside of the house and the barns. Hay bales had been arranged as seats all over the place and they had even built a hay bale cave, complete with a tunnel entrance. Great! I remember that after we'd watched Starsky and Hutch, there was music playing throughout the house and garden, though whether it was a proper disco or not I don't recall. Along with the lemonade and coca cola,

Damaged Goods

we had some other bottles that we had liberated, so there were a few of us merrier than the rest!

The night seemed to go on and on. Like the heat. I went for a walk round the barns and sat chatting to a blonde girl on a hay bale. She was a few years older than me and very pretty, or so she looked that night anyway. We chatted for a bit and she said she wanted to see the tree house. We walked hand in hand across the dry ploughed field and clambered up the ladder. When we got up inside, she grabbed hold of me and pulled me to her. Blimey! I began to give her a big French kiss, just like I'd learned on holiday. Except that it went on for a bit longer. She seemed to like it, as we snogged and sort of fumbled around for ages, not really getting anywhere, but it was fun that's for sure.

We finally gave up and returned to the party about an hour later. Now I knew what all the fuss was about and felt very grown up. I never saw her again and for some reason that was also the last time I went to stay with my friend there too, after all those years. We were at that age where we were changing schools and finding different sets of friends I guess, but I missed him.

I went back to see their house a few years ago, long after he had grown up and left home and they had moved away to a Penthouse by the Thames in London. Probably shouldn't have. The old house still looked massive, but the tree house was gone, all but a few rotten planks hanging down. Tempus fugit and all that.

I hardly saw any of my old friends anymore in the term time, I was miles away at school 6 days a week. Was this how being grown up was going to be? I didn't fancy it much really, to be honest. Couldn't see the point.

The long hot summer was finally coming to an end and I was back to my new school. Bedford. My brother was there in the year above me and had got on well, as in spite of being a bit troublesome he was good at school work. I wasn't and I soon hated it. Mum or Dad gave us a lift to the train station and after a 40 minute journey, it was a mile and a half walk through the town, five and a half days a week! It was all boys and felt like being in a prison camp to me. My winter escape already seemed like a lifetime ago.

So there I was, summoned to Taff's office after school finished on Saturday, before my detention, for the heinous crime of not having handed in my homework. My form master was in the office too, to gloat I suppose - fat oily haired bastard. Taff was my maths teacher, as well as the rugby coach - all 18 stone of him. His eyes were alight as he intoned his favourite phrase, something to do with 'skylarking about.'

Over the chair and out with his cane - not your average bamboo stick, but the type of thing most inadequate men buy a big red E type for. It was over an inch in diameter, and he pivoted round on his toes, twisting at the waist to give that little bit more oomph. I had three then, all the while my form master looking at me excitedly. Fuck that hurt.

When he had finished, he said something about hoping he wouldn't have to do it again, but his face gave lie to his words. I looked him in the eye and did not cry; I held my breath and bit down on my bottom lip until I left that room, and then half way down the stairs I broke down. I don't know how I managed to sit on a chair later that afternoon, for the whole 2 hour detention.

It was a full week until my mother caught sight of my legs and backside, by then scabbed, and black with bruising. She forgave me for having thrown away my trousers, when she realised that I had done it because they were caked in blood.

I think it could have been worse though. There was another teacher who we all called Queenie, who wore a yellow

Damaged Goods

tracksuit and new fangled yellow Adidas trainers. He was in charge of P.E. and known to be a bit of a perv,' with no handstand safe from his groping and no class safe from his leering smile in the changing rooms. He could often be seen in the summer, walking naked around the outdoor pool during the swimming lesson, rubbing himself vigorously with a small towel. It was rumoured that he gave his own form of special attention to one or two of the boys, though no one was quite sure who, or when. Somehow, I preferred the dumb brutality of Taff to Queenie's attentions, whatever they might have been.

I spent my days counting down the hours 'til I could go back to sleep and it seemed like there was nothing good in my waking world anymore. It was 1977, I was 12 years old and that was a dark path to be on.

It was around then that I started stealing anything that wasn't nailed down. Records and books and stuff from the shops in town, the odd pound or two from my parents room, anything really and though I seemed to be good at it, it was just for the excitement as far as I was concerned. Something that made me feel alive.

One Saturday on the way home from school, I went into a little shop just off the high street, that had a gents barbers upstairs, which all the boys used, to get a haircut. It closed at 2 on Saturdays but it was only about half past one, so I should be all right. The proprietor, who ran both businesses, was busy serving someone in the shop and so I just went on upstairs and sat down.

There was a table with magazines on it and a rack full of golden oldie 45rpm's which were for sale. I sat there reading and then browsing through the records, until I looked at my watch and realised it was quarter past two.

All of a sudden it seemed awfully quiet, so I listened for a while but still couldn't hear anything. Hadn't he seen me? I got up and went down stairs, only to find that the lights were off and the shop was empty. Oh dear. I tried the front door and found it locked, walked behind the counter through into the back room and found the same with the back door. I was locked in!

Hmm. I stood there and thought about what to do and how I could get out, but it wasn't long before the possibilities hit me.

I went back upstairs and looked around. I knew from my previous visits that the till was just a wooden drawer with a bell that pinged when you opened it, so I slowly slid it open, the ping of the little bell sounding deafening in the silence. I froze and held my breath, still thinking that someone would appear from somewhere, but they didn't.

There was a large stack of pound notes and fivers sitting there right in front of my eyes, held down under a spring clip and I gingerly slid a handful out. I thought it was best not to be too greedy, so I stuffed them in my pocket and closed the draw. As I picked up my case I noticed the records again. Well, it would be a shame not to take full advantage of my situation, so I hurriedly stuffed a few of them into my case while I was at it as well. My heart was pounding and my legs felt wobbly, I had never thought of actually robbing anywhere, but here I was, the third Kray Twin. Now I just had to get away with it!

The upstairs room had a sash window over a small ledge, which stuck out over the shop front below and from there it was only about an eight feet drop down to the pavement.

Crouching down out of sight, I slowly slid it up and peered out over the windowsill. I could see the traffic going along the high street, but the side road I was in was empty. I clambered carefully out onto the ledge, turning round to close the window behind me and dropped my case onto the pavement, before lowering myself down and dropping the last few feet. I picked up my case and walked off, trying to look innocent, expecting someone to shout or something, but nobody did – Blimey, I'd done it!

Even though I was excited, I tried to think like a master criminal and was very careful not to tell anyone what I'd done, or spend the money in large amounts and it lasted

Damaged Goods

me for ages. I never went back in that shop though, just in case.

Another thing we got away with at that school was a wood pigeon. We were taught Religious Education by a vicar, who had white hair and an unfortunately high pitched voice. Sometimes, before the lesson, one of us would climb up and hide in the fir tree outside his window and when he started, would shout things out in an equally high pitched voice. He would get so angry at not being able to find the culprit, that his face would go bright red and his voice went higher and higher, until it ended up being just a screech, poor bloke.

One day, we had found a dead wood pigeon in the tree by his window and brought it in and hid it, on top of the big drop down projector screen at the back of his classroom. After a week or two, the smell was awful and it got steadily worse over that term, much to the disdain and annoyance of the vicar.

Unfortunately we had to put up with it too, so it didn't turn out to be so funny after all. It was gone after the holidays though, so someone must have found it.

Another Saturday and I was in detention, again. It seemed like it was getting to be every week and I never really understood exactly what I did to deserve them all. Perhaps fighting in the playground and not doing much work didn't help. I couldn't really see the point. My parents seemed so wrapped up in their lives that they hardly noticed me, though it has to be said that wasn't necessarily a bad thing.

I tried telling them that I wanted to be a writer or an actor, but they just kept telling me it was about time I got my head down and did some hard work, like they did. For what? Did they honestly think that I wanted to end up like them? It wasn't likely, we had very little in common, unsurprisingly, and nor did I want to have. I saw where their lifetime of hard work had got them and for all the things they had achieved, like the big house, cars and invites to the Palace, where Dad took my sisters to garden parties, I decided that it sure wasn't the life that I wanted. I guess it's almost normal for kids not to understand their parents and vice versa, but even if I'd known that then it wouldn't have helped – this was my life and I couldn't see beyond it.

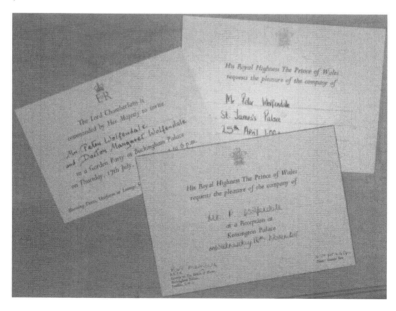

By Royal Invitation!

Damaged Goods

Donna Summer was all over the radio singing 'I Feel Love' and at least it sounded like someone was having a damned good time, somewhere. I couldn't wait to be older.

At school I had to do rugby and rowing, which wasn't that bad. In fact I quite liked rowing in a scull on the river or the boating lake, though it always seemed to be freezing if you fell in and wasn't like The Broads.

In rugby, I liked the tackling and I could at least run fast when I got the ball and made the most of that whenever I got the chance. Unfortunately though, having to be there on Saturdays to play, soon killed what little enthusiasm I had for either sport.

Going to see Luton play West Ham with my brother one weekend and standing in the Oak Road stand, amongst tall, flat cap wearing, roll up smoking men for an hour and a half, trying to see the game through the drizzle finally put me off football too.

Walking back through the town after my detentions in my uniform, I may as well have been wearing a target. The boys from Pilgrim's, the comprehensive down the road, always looked out for us for a bit of sport. They had found me the week before, four of them. I'd fought as hard as I could, but there were four of them and they gave me a right hiding, nothing too bad, but it hurt and I'd cut all the knuckles open on my right hand, which swelled up like a balloon.

I was ready that week though. All week long, in metalwork, I had for once been busy. A piece of aluminium tubing, for which I had made plugs on the lathe, both hammered in and filled with sand. Nice. I'd even polished it. Ready I was.

I'd got nearly as far as St John's railway station, when there they were. 'Oi snob!' they shouted. I kept walking, giving them a chance to give up. I half hoped that they would, as I knew where it would lead. They didn't. I heard the sound of their DM's as they ran up behind me and it was too late. Bollocks. Okay then, here we go.

'Who's a fuckin' snob now then?' I shouted as I turned, weapon in my hand. It was like a film. They somehow froze in midstep. Bad move. I ran the few yards between us and slashed at the biggest one, just catching his arm, then crashed the club down on the next nearest one's shoulder.

I wasn't the scared one that week and wouldn't be again either. They screamed and shouted, the other two taking off at a sprint, not wanting to risk it to help their mates. My would-be attackers were crying. I stood still and told them to fuck off and never come near me again, or I'd kill them. I think they got the message. I never had any more trouble from them whilst I was at that school, though I managed to find plenty more, all by myself, at school and at home.

Another boy from our school, who went on the same train as me, started to bring in bottles of drink on Saturday mornings, as his parents owned an off licence and it was easy for him to slip the odd half bottle into his bag. We shared it amongst 3 or 4 of us and it was usually vodka, which didn't leave much of a smell on our breath.

On Saturdays, we had double design and technology first, which was in a long converted attic room, where we always made sure we sat the furthest from the teacher. This was followed by break time and then P.E., which, as it was summer, meant swimming in Queenie's outdoor pool. Somehow no one ever noticed that we were all half pissed.

My young drinking came to an abrupt end when he gave me a half bottle of whisky though. No one else liked it on the train, so I took it home. That evening down the rec,' I proceeded to drink most of it myself and got very, very drunk. To start with the rest of the gang thought it was funny, but I soon became somewhat comatose. When he saw how ill I had got, my brother, in his inimitable style, tried giving me a smack in the mouth and putting my head under the tap outside the cricket pavilion, but it did nothing to sober me up. I was hammered.

Damaged Goods

I stumbled up the hill, somehow making it home, mumbling at Mum that I was going to bed as I staggered up to my room. It was still light and only teatime. I spent that night, with a worried mother looking on, as I proceeded to throw up out of my bedroom window for hours. I didn't enjoy that feeling or the bollocking I got the next day, so I steered clear of drinking for a while after that.

Anyway, back to that Saturday. I was home by half two. Just as well. I was supposed to meet my friends, to go through the woods to Stockgrove Park with the village gang. A couple of weeks before, one of our lot had been down there on his own and a load of boys from the borstal that was there in those days, had given him a right kicking. We'd gone back the following week and found three of them. We roughed them up a bit and told them to tell the rest we'd all be there the next week, for a proper showdown.

I hid my club in my jacket and set off, but I was 20 minutes late and they had left the Rec' already. I ran all the way through the woods, finally catching up with them down at the far end of the lake. What an army!

There were 12 of us from our village and about 30 others from the 6th form of Leon school, down in the town. There were all sorts of weapons, sheath knives, penknives, an old bayonet, spiked chains from a fence, someone even bought along a single boxing glove. And sticks, loads of big heavy sticks from the woods. We weren't there to prove anything and we weren't there to make threats. We were there to teach the borstal boys a lesson they wouldn't forget. We'd show them what ganging up was really like.

In the event, the biggest and eldest of us, who was 16 and eldest brother to the one who originally got beaten up, decided that sticks would be enough. We had to dump the rest in the brambles and I never did go back to find my club. We went to a hill near the borstal and everyone got down and hid in the ferns. Except for me, Jam and two others, the youngest there - we stood up and waited. We didn't have to wait long. They started to arrive at the bottom of the hill in dribs and drabs, until finally there were about 20 of them. Right, here we go then. We started shouting down at them to come up and get us, then started throwing sticks and that was it. They charged up the hill. Twats.

We stood our ground, and like a general in a war film, our leader made everyone wait until they were almost upon us, then 30 or so big boys, with big sticks, suddenly stood up and our enemies froze. The look on their faces as they realised just how fucked they were, was hilarious. Well, it was from where we were standing.

They tried to turn and run back down, but we were on them. Kicking, punching screaming, they shat themselves. They stumbled down the hill and ran back towards the borstal, picking themselves up as we knocked them down again like skittles. We headed some of them off towards the lake and two of them got caught in a bog. Standing there defenceless, up to their knees, suddenly they didn't look so tough. I wasn't a bully, they obviously didn't want to fight anymore and it wouldn't be any fun now, so we left them there. After making them take their boots out of the bog and throw them into the woods.

We chased the rest all the way back to the Borstal and they ran in through the big gate in the fence, out of which suddenly appeared the headmaster.

'Go home boys' he shouted.

'Fuck off!' we all shouted back.

He slammed the gate shut and peered through it. We began to rain our sticks and stones and insults over the fence, determined to get them all somehow, until eventually, the headmaster shouted that he'd called the police. We'd run out of things to throw anyway, so we disappeared off back into the woods, still shouting obscenities. We all felt like a conquering army - Great!

Unfortunately, three nights later, the police appeared at my mum and dad's house, which wasn't so great. No, that

Damaged Goods

didn't go down well at all. For all the fun of the moment though, somewhere I knew my life was fucked.

At home it always seemed to be winter. Dad was going out a lot and the atmosphere was not good. I guess I didn't help, but who was affecting who? It felt like a whirlpool that I couldn't get out of.

After my 'boxing experience' down the rec' and watching David Carradine on the TV, I'd started kung fu lessons and was loving it, after a few months. My brother bought one of his friends home from school one weekend. He was big for his age and usually alright with me, like another of my brother's friend Pigsy, but he could be a bit of a bully sometimes.

We were down the rec' when he started picking on me. Probably bored, sitting on the swings. He went to kick me in the balls and I moved to one side and caught his outstretched leg and pulled. It flipped him straight onto his back. I kept hold of his ankle, twisting it to keep him down. It looked like I knew what I was doing, which wasn't quite true, but he didn't know that. I shouted at him to pick on someone his own size and leave me the fuck alone. I turned and walked away and he shouted a few obscenities after me, but neither him nor my brother came after me. Spoilt the rest of my day though and I wasn't friends with him after that. Why do things always have to end like that?

Apart from raids on the dairy, I'm sorry to say that we'd sometimes go into the little village shop and pinch whatever we could find. All the sweets were behind the counter, so we just took whatever stuff we could reach and hide under our jumpers, before the shopkeeper came in from the back room. Just the odd thing, it was just for the thrill of it really, but it made us feel like proper little gangsters.

Sometimes too, me and my brother would get up really early in the morning and sneak off down to the private trout lake in the woods, with little red and white 2 piece fishing rods from Woolworths. We'd sit and pull loads of the fat, lazy fish out of the water without too much trouble, then pop them in carrier bags and take them up the hill and sell them to my nanny's husband.

Damaged Goods

On one occasion, we bumped into a stranger who seemed not quite right and proceeded to trip me up and kick seven bells out of me, before my brother chased him off. Another time we met a nutter who proceeded to shout at us and pulled a knife. My brother braved it out whilst I sprinted up the lane and got my Uncle Malc and his Dad, who came back and showed the guy what being scared was really all about. We weren't always so lucky though.

There was one Saturday when there were seven or eight of us, including my brother and Jam, playing Cowboys and Indians down in the woods, with bows and arrows we'd made with our sheath knives. 4 men appeared out of the bushes in front of us, all with air rifles. They threatened us, taking our knives and stamping on our bows and arrows to break them. After roughing us up a bit, they said that if we tried to run they'd kill us, and bury us in the mud. We believed them as they put us up against trees and shot at us. We were only little and scared shitless. We tried vainly to escape, finally making it, but even then they shot at our heels as we fled in all directions. The police got involved after our parents found out what had happened and I heard that some of the men went to prison.

Guns and close calls seemed to figure a lot in our childhood, one way and another. One evening me and Jam were down at a friend's house, just hanging out, reading comics and smoking. The friend whose house it was had a.22 target pistol that we'd been out in the garden with earlier, shooting at tin cans and stuff.

I was sitting on his bed, reading a Beano annual, when Jam picked up the pistol and pointed it at me. Without thinking anything of it I held up the annual, just as he pulled the trigger. None of us remembered that it was still loaded. The shot went right through both covers of the hardback book and hit me in the neck. It felt like someone had punched me and I fell back on the bed. The room went quiet and Jam stood there, as shocked as I was.

I sat up slowly and felt my neck, and wincing, pulled the little piece of lead out, leaving a perfect round hole, out of which blood started to trickle. I couldn't believe it. 'You shot me' was all I could say. Jam said he was sorry and someone else went and got some toilet roll and a plaster, to cover it up.

Panic over, I wasn't dead. I did my best to be tough about it and pretend it didn't hurt, but bugger, it did. I was ok though, just had a nasty bruise, along with a little cut that soon healed in a week or two. I bet there aren't many people who had their life saved by a Beano annual and I learnt, as we all did that night, not to point a real gun at someone unless you mean it.

Me and my friend Dave went down to the private trout lake alone one winter, to find it frozen solid. We threw a few sticks to make sure, then ventured out onto the ice, skating around on our heels.

It seemed fine and we thought we'd walk right across it, until we got about 20ft from the shore and it started to crack with a loud pinging noise. A crack was coming from the edge, zigzagging towards us. We ran the other way, which was further, but at least we were escaping the crack. It followed us, pinging, all the way to the far shore and as we jumped off the ice, a large sheet of it slowly tilted up into the air, before sliding noiselessly back down into the cold dark water in slow motion. Blimey, that was close.

Dave played the saxophone and sometimes tried to kid everyone that he was Canadian. He also had a very strict Mum. One afternoon she wouldn't let him out to play and I remember my brother writing on their house, in big chalk letters for all the world to see, that she was a C**t! I couldn't believe he'd done it. Always fearless my brother, he wasn't scared of grownups or consequences.

Mum and Dad had converted one of our garages into a big playroom for us and after a while, all the village boys and girls used to come and hang out there in the evenings. We had our old Binatone record player set up in there and used to sit listening to Thin Lizzy and Queen, on some big old bus seats from my Nanny's husband, that we used as sofas. We often still had bottles of fizzy drink from the dairy and used to open one of the big doors when we wanted to

Damaged Goods

smoke. After a particularly bad row with his mum and dad one day, my friend Dave came to live in our garage for a month or two. I thought it was great having him as a lodger, he had his own kettle in there and everything. Very cool. He'd come and eat with us all at mealtimes and stuff though and he used to play along on his Saxophone, if we put Gerry Rafferty's 'Baker Street' or some Joan Armatrading album on.

Mum and Dad seemed to like him being there too, he seemed very grown up and we'd sit and talk about the meaning of life until late at night, smoking his roll ups. Eventually, when things had calmed down with his parents, he moved back home, before leaving the village to go off to college. I was sorry to see him go and I guess a bit jealous really, as I was still there. I really wanted to be older.

It was around that time that Punk Rock became big news. On Top of The Pops, there was Fox singing 'S-S-Single Bed,' which seemed very risqué to me, the sort of thing that would make my parents squirm, when all of a sudden there was the Marc Bolan show on ITV with The Damned singing 'New Rose,' which blew it right out of the water. Yes!

One day, my brother had come home from school with spiky, bright orange hair and had an almighty argument with mum and dad. I could hear his records, like Patti Smith's 'Because The Night' and The Adverts 'No Time To Be 21' blaring angrily from his room at night, and I soaked up every chord and line.

He'd come home full of stories of gigs that he'd been to, the same bands that I heard on the radio. The year before, I had seen The Sex Pistols swearing at Bill Grundy on the TV at teatime, before my dad hurriedly turned it off and I started to listen to the John Peel show on my transistor radio. Snuggled up under the blankets, in the days before duvets arrived, that too was full of punk. The Saints, The Damned, The Clash, Xray Spex and suddenly it seemed I wasn't the only one angry at life. This new music seemed to know just how I felt.

Sometimes, when he wasn't there, I used to 'borrow' my brother's bondage trousers to go out in, much to his annoyance and dreamed of having some of my own. I cut the sleeves off my faded denim jacket and drew a big razor blade on the back instead, covering the front with safety pins, even putting one through my ear, which my Nanny had pierced for me the month before with a hot needle. That was it, I was going to be a punk.

Sid Vicious died in the spring, a long way from home, almost like he'd gone all the way to the States just to find his sad destiny. What a waste I thought. A few months later, one evening I was lying in a hammock at the bottom of the garden, having a sneaky fag and listening to radio Luxembourg, when they announced that Elvis Presley had died. The DJ was crying and I couldn't quite believe it. I

Damaged Goods

loved all his records and films and he had always seemed untouchable and immortal to me.

Then, a few months later, Marc Bolan died too. He had always been the brightest star of Glam and I was just as upset by him leaving. That same year, Maria Callas and Bing Crosby, Joan Crawford, Groucho Marx and Charlie Chaplin also died. Blimey, they were dropping like flies. I guess that was the first time that I noticed famous people dying. It seemed like my old record collection and favourite old films were becoming full of ghosts and I began to realise that nothing lasted for ever. Their passing seemed to bring an era already over to a close and I wondered who was I going to look up to now? It sounded like punk was out there waiting for me now and maybe that was what I had been looking for.

There wasn't a whole lot for a teenager to do in the village and by that time, cigarettes had started to fill any empty spaces in my day and give me a couple of minutes escape from myself.

When I'd had my first few, I was only about 8 or 9 and didn't really know what I was supposed to feel. The hard, sharp taste and smell was new, the older kids egging me on, saying if I didn't take it in I was a poof and all that kind of stuff. I thought I looked cool and big if I'm honest, but as I stood there trying not to cough, I guess I would've looked like a stupid little boy really.

My Mum was a cancer doctor and had always warned me against it, but we were going to be young forever and health just didn't come into it. Cigarettes became my friend. Unfortunately, they start out filling your time and end up stealing it from you, with every breath. I found out when I was older that it's not a good idea to have friends that'll kill you, but I didn't know that then.

If we couldn't scrounge one, we'd pool our pocket money and one of us would go to the little side door at the pub and buy ten Number 6 and a box of matches, saying they were for one of the older boys. It worked well enough for me, until one day, the older boy whose name I gave had been and bought a pack of twenty a few minutes before. Ooops!

Damaged Goods

Me and Jam went camping with my Mum and Dad in Devon for a week. We all drove down there in Dad's Volvo estate, with the back seats down and us two lying across the luggage. Dad thought he was being very modern by tuning the radio to Johnnie Walker on radio 2 for us, but it still sounded like a load of oldies to us. We had our own tent and we thought it was a proper adventure. We went down to the sea front and played on the beach most days, which was great, but we did have to go for the odd walk along the coast with Mum and Dad.

In the evenings we'd get a lift into town and arrange where and when to be picked up later on. One night, after we finally managed to find a pub that would serve us, we sat down with our pints of cider, on a bench by the fireplace. It turned out that a punky looking girl sat next to us only lived about 20 miles from us back at home, holidays can be weird like that. We chatted away ten to the dozen all night.

The landlady had a cigar stub in the corner of her mouth and a bad twitch in her eye. We thought that she looked like a pirate and the more drinks we had, the funnier she looked. I kept telling Jam that she was winking at him and we all got the drunken giggles, endlessly. Luckily she ignored us and let us get on with it and we had a great time until it was time to go.

When Dad came to pick us up, I asked if I could get on the roof rack of his Volvo estate. Must have been all that cider. To my surprise and sudden concern he said yes, but it was too late to back out now. I clambered up and lay there on top of the car, holding on to the front rail.

It was windy little back lanes all the way to the campsite, so there wasn't any other traffic and Dad really put his foot down. I swung from side to side as he flew round the bends in the dark and was very glad when we finally got back and stopped. Dad got out and as I got down he asked if I'd enjoyed my ride. I tried not to wobble and look unruffled as I said that I had but he went faster than I expected. He laughed and said that I'd have only moaned if he went slowly. Me and my big mouth. I guess he was right though!

After what seemed like forever, the old Teddy boy finally gave up DJ'ing at the village disco. In his place a big farmer type guy, Mark, who lived in a cottage, down by the 'S' bends and played cricket for the village, took over. He had a big black Transit van and me and Jam started to get there early, to help him unload all his boxes of records, wanting even the faintest connection to the entertainment world.

Like the old Ted, he played all the latest releases. He had a penchant for rock music and was quite happy to play our punk singles if we brought them along, though he also seemed to have a large stock of his own. At that age I couldn't afford all the latest punk gear, but that wasn't a problem, my old needlework classes came in handy and I just sat in my room, copied the shirts and jackets and made my own, which I thought looked great. Sometimes though I'd just wear pyjamas and safety pins, it didn't matter, that was the fun of it. We'd pogo away, to The Banshees, The Pistols and The Clash, our chains and straps chinking as we all jumped about.

At the end of the night, James Last was replaced by the Bee Gees 'How Deep is Your Love?' or 'Hopelessly Devoted To You' from Grease, which some girls I knew went to see 6 times in a row. Mark was a great DJ though and I thought he was very cool with all of us lot and the disco's continued to be just brilliant and as popular as ever.

One Saturday, me and Jam saw him doing some concreting, by the cricket nets at the 'rec. After sitting watching and talking about it for a couple of hours, we plucked up courage and went and asked him if he needed a hand and if we could have a job. He stopped and looked at us for a while, then said that if we wanted to, we could mix the cement on his board and bring it over to him in the wheelbarrow. If we were any good, he'd see about the next weekend and decide how much he was going to pay us. Yes! I had my first proper job. He did landscape gardening and I worked for Mark nearly every weekend and holiday from that day, until I was about 17.

I cut a thousand lawns and banks, with old mowers that were always going wrong and dug a thousand holes with

Damaged Goods

old spades and shovels. I also got to use axes, chainsaws and flamethrowers, drove ride on mowers, tractors and even his van in the end, usually badly!

He always had some old rock cassette playing in his van, Cream, Hendrix, Free or something and I got a real musical education in what was and what wasn't considered any good by grownups.

We worked hard, often from dawn 'til dusk, stopping only for the odd cup of tea and to go to a cafe for lunch. We always went and had a pint in the village pub at the end of the day and I loved it. His wages gave me some freedom and independence of a sort and bought me all my punk gear, and all the records, beer and cigarettes that I wanted.

He was also the first person to make me feel like I was worth anything. He told me that I was just as good as anyone else and that I could do, or be, anything that I wanted to, even if I didn't do well at school.

That was a revelation and I never knew what to say really, I felt far from believing him, but it was a real turnaround to hear a grown up say those things to me.

I never did get caught for shoplifting and the only time I ever involved anyone else in my thieving, was the last time. He grassed me up and I got suspended from Bedford School and never went back, a bit of a foregone conclusion by the time it happened. My poor Dad had to come and pick me up from the Headmaster's office and that was one of those times when sorry just wasn't enough.

The understandable trouble I got into at home for that finally cured my light fingeredness, but apart from that, the only good thing I had achieved there was to win the Phillpotts English Literature Prize for my stories, out of the whole 2,000 boys.

For my winning story I had read the book 'Jaws' and kind of copied the style that it was written in. My English teacher had persuaded the headmaster that both it and all my other writing was promising and I owe him a debt of gratitude for that.

My mum and dad never came to the big presentation ceremony and you could see that the headmaster didn't want me to have it, but fuck him, my writing was good and I smiled as he handed over the inscribed book I'd won as a prize. I still have it.

I gather that both Taff and Queenie were sacked a year or two later as well, with there being no place for them in a school trying to move out of the stone age. The great hall there was burned down too, in an attack of mindless arson. Now ain't that a shame.

Damaged Goods

I was sent, in shame, to the senior part of my previous school, who luckily still remembered me fondly. I should have been grateful and made the most of it, but I wasn't and I didn't.

It had moved to an old mansion up in the woods, a few miles from home and I had to cycle there and back, which I didn't mind. I started in the autumn though and there was snow after Christmas. When I saw Mum and Dad cruising past me in their new Rover, as I pushed my bike up the steep hill, slipping in the snow and feeling very sorry for myself, I knew it was all my fault and that I had run out of chances with them.

Sometimes after school, a friend would give me a tow home on my pushbike. He had a little Yamaha FS1e and I held on to his outstretched arm as we sped along the back roads at 20 or 30 mph. It never felt any more dangerous than the go karts we'd had when we were little, that my Nanny's husband made for us and on which we used to burn all the way down the hill, round the corner by the pub, and down the lane to the woods. I guess it probably was though.

The one best thing about that school, was that after all the restrictions of Bedford, it had girls, loads of them. I felt like a kid in a sweetshop and loved them all, even the lady teachers. The other children were all ok and I don't think I had one fight with anyone else during my time there, though I did get into someone else's once.

One of my schoolmates had been beaten up by some of the lads who lived near the school. We arranged to meet them in the woods for a punch up to settle it. Oh goody, I had done this before! There were about equal numbers of us when we met and faced each other, under the trees at the bottom of our sports field.

One thing that I guessed wasn't going to be equal, was the fact that I had brought from home with me that day, a large piece of heavy chain which I had hidden under my jacket, wrapped around my waist and a small axe that I shoved under my coat.

The fight started, my classmate squaring up against their biggest and without delay they started on each other. It was a fierce fight, with kicks to the head and everything. When my classmate began to get the upper hand, all the other lot moved to join in and help their mate. I shouted at them 'That's enough!' and pulled the chain and axe from under my coat. 'Whoa' they shouted, 'There's no need for that mate.' I told them there fuckin' well was from where I was standing, and that if they wanted some, or touched my mate again, I'd do the lot of them. Wankers.

The way I saw it, the only mistake I made that day was to show the axe to one of the younger boys at our school, when I was getting my bike out of the bike shed later on to go home. He was scared by it and told his teacher, who told the headmaster. I guess it came out like I had tried to scare him, which wasn't true, but my headmaster didn't know that. He had however known me on and off since I was 8 and knew that I was no bully.

Though he was old and small in stature, he could be very scary when he wanted to be. He had been a Lt. Colonel with the Ghurkhas in the war and I got an almighty, righteous, bollocking from him, worthy of any parade ground and that was that. We never had any more trouble with that other lot of boys though, funnily enough.

Whilst I was there, the school had a Disco at the end of term. The boy with the little Yamaha had a cousin who was in a band and they were booked to play. Me and about five others turned up in our punk gear, much to the annoyance of the teachers. This became even funnier when the band came on. They were a full on punk band, called The Phasers, complete with a Joy Division style singer. After the disco had played ELO, Elvis Costello and all the usual suspects, they came on and played a storming set, with us lot jumping about and pogoing for all we were worth. They were brilliant.

Damaged Goods

I spoke to them afterwards and realised that you didn't have to be famous to be in a band, I decided that I wanted to do that too, though I had no idea who with.

At the start of the next term, I went to see Dexy's Midnight Runners in concert with a friend from school. I was amazed that a band that wasn't punk or Heavy Metal could be so loud. Kevin Rowland was a masterful, powerful front man, with the rest of the band being note perfect and looking and sounding very heavy.

Over the next few years, gigs became a big part of my life and I went to hundreds, The Clash, The Police, The Ruts, Stiff Little Fingers, Adam and The Ants and all the other bands around at that time. Sometimes they were local, sometimes we'd all bunk a train to see them in London, but they were all always worth the journey there, even though it sometimes ended up in me walking miles home afterwards.

One that I walked 14 miles home from was The Clash playing at Aylesbury Friar's. It was a real standout gig amongst all the others and they had Ian Dury and The Blockheads as their Special Mystery Guests.

They did a storming set, with Ian Dury standing at the microphone pulling scarves out of his pocket like a magician and after they'd finished, we all chanted for the Blockheads to come back on, right into the first Clash song, so much so that they did and played a few numbers with the Clash, with Ian Dury blowing his Harmonica for all he was worth. Both bands were at the top of their game at that time and it was a brilliant, brilliant night, worth every penny and every mile.

Nights after school in the week had got lonely in the village now. At night, I would often find myself sitting alone in the church porch having a fag, rather than sitting alone in my bedroom. Smoking was company, of a sort and wasn't that what people did in the films when they were lonely, or needed to think? That's what I did anyway.

I was walking back from town in the rain one day in my best punk outfit, when a yellow Cortina flew past, blaring it's horn, and someone shouting 'Oi Punky!' I stuck my fingers up and shouted at them to fuck off. Ooops.

The car skidded to a halt, then reversed back and stopped. The driver got out and asked me who I thought I was sticking my fingers up at. His mates in the car laughed when I replied 'You, you c**t.' I guess it was funny coming from someone younger than them, but the driver didn't think so. He squared up to me and threw a punch at my face, I hopped backwards then threw one back at him. Now he laughed. 'Fuck me boys, we've got a right little tough nut here' he shouted out.

As he turned to look at his mates I gave him a good one on the side of his jaw, which caught him by surprise. He was not amused. He gave me an almighty left hook, which caught me in the ribs, making a sickening crack. As he went to deliver another haymaker, I shot out a right cross at his face, as hard as I could, but it was to no avail. His punch caught me right in the solar plexus, lifting me off of my feet.

I dropped to my hands and knees retching, trying to breathe as he stood there, laughing. His mates in the car were laughing at both of us now. They got out and came over, just in time to stop him from giving me more than the one kick he already had. 'Come on' they said 'He's only little, leave him alone.' He looked down at me and managed to chuckle through his grimace, before walking back to his car and driving off, beeping his horn. After they'd gone, I sat at the side of the road, gingerly feeling my side, glad that none of my mates had been there to see it and decided that I wouldn't be sticking my fingers up at any more cars anytime soon. That rib hurt for weeks.

Damaged Goods

I remember being very upset when my brother came home one day, dressed in a shiny suit and wearing loafers, with a Secret Affair album stuffed under his new parka. He was a Mod! He said that punk was dead and anyway, it wasn't the clothes that were important, or even the music really, just the attitude. I couldn't quite see it, it was more than just a fashion wasn't it? I didn't want something new, I still wanted to experience all the stuff he'd told me about, I felt cheated.

I don't know if it was me, but even the TV shows which used to offer exciting glimpses of America, like Kojak, Starsky and Hutch and the like, had begun to seem less exciting. Everything was getting mixed up and the fun being replaced with something darker. I had heard about a film called the Texas Chainsaw Massacre and even that sounded like an X rated version of Scooby Doo. So wasn't America like it was shown on the TV either then? What about The Fonz and Happy Days? Surely there had to be somewhere over the rainbow. Even pop music wasn't what it had been. Glam rock was well and truly over and the fun seemed to have gone out of the charts.

The remains of punk filtered through to the mainstream, 'New Wave' they called it. Our common room at school always seemed to be playing Blondie, or Rainbow, or Devo or something, but I wondered, had TV and the radio been lying to me all along? Buggles sang about Video killing the radio star and life just didn't seem that simple anymore.

One Saturday morning I'd gone to town with my dad and was sitting in my punk gear on a bench in the rec,' whilst he was at his factory, when a familiar looking elder punk came up and spoke to me. He asked where I was from and told me to come to a pub later, where all the local punks hung out.

I'd seen him jogging through the woods a couple of times, when I was out running, thinking I was Kwai Chang Caine. His name was Tony and he was a boxer. I didn't go then as

I was still too young to go to pubs and anyway had no way of getting there. It sure sounded exciting though.

Damaged Goods

I was asked to leave that school as well in the end, I hadn't done anything really bad, apart from sneaking off into the woods for a smoke or a snog, but I hadn't done much work or been a shining example of anything either, so, with resigned looks on their faces, my Mum and Dad found me another place and I changed schools again.

Understandably, their choices in that department were becoming somewhat limited and with 1 year left to go, I was sent to the sixth form at the comprehensive in town.

It was there that I met another young punk, who knew all the rest from town and I started to hang out with them, finally going to that pub and making friends with Tony and all the rest of them. What a gang!

There were punks, skinheads, mods, soulboys and loads of girls. Great! There seemed to be an endless supply of parties and new people to meet. I went with them all to see the local big punk band that Tony played drums for, The Chronic Outbursts, at the town youth club. Along with UK Decay from Luton was their supporting act, The Statics, who my brother used to play bass for. They had a gorgeous punk girl playing guitar for them, who sometimes played bass for UK Decay as well.

Wow, what a gig that was! All the bands were absolutely brilliant. Afterwards I copied The Statics logo and painted it on the back of my leather jacket and went to see them play at every opportunity.

They were the best as far as I was concerned, everything about them screamed success, from their songs to their looks, but somehow they never made the big time, it was UK Decay instead. Shame. Has to be said that UK Decay were great too though, still are, just different.

Me and my Statics Jacket, 1979.

Girls, music, clothes and staying away from home. I had found a place and a group of people who were all outsiders, for one reason or another and for the first time in my life, I had found somewhere that I fitted in and I didn't feel so alone anymore. It wasn't like the movies, but it sure was somewhere different.

We all used to go to gigs at the Compass club, where after 'Jah Lizard's New Wave Disco' there were sometimes famous punk/new wave bands and sometimes local ones, including The Phasers, the remains of whom still play now, as The Peartree Bridge Family, as well as UK Decay, The Statics and all the usual suspects.

It was funny when The Chronic Outbursts used to play there and a fight broke out between the two town's punks and skinheads, as because my village was situated between the two, I knew them all so I never joined in, which made a nice change.

Damaged Goods

A new punk friend of mine, Andy, lodged with this guy and his girlfriend, in a little house on the far side of town. It was painted in Rasta colours and he was always playing Bob Marley, or Bowie, or Iggy Pop.

One night I went with them to a party on the 12th floor of the town's only tower block. It was full of older druggies and I saw, for the first time, someone in the kitchen injecting themselves with a golden liquid. That scared me.

Going back out into the front room, I bumped into an older American boy, who I had known from Bedford school. He was surprised to see me there and was that night, the first person to ever offer me a spliff. Not knowing or understanding what to do, I took it and proceeded to smoke the whole thing, as they looked on, grinning. They thought it was hilarious. It didn't really hit me straight away and I hadn't noticed the time passing when suddenly, feeling distinctly unwell, I got up and said I had to go and get picked up by my Dad. I made it as far as outside their door, onto the landing, before I keeled over and fainted, just before I got to the top of the stairwell. They were all suddenly very concerned and picked me up and carried me back inside, putting a wet towel on my face, before sitting me on a chair by the open window.

After about twenty minutes, the American ended up giving me a lift to meet my Dad, by which time I had straightened out sufficiently for him not to notice the state I was in. Phew!

Another time, someone gave me a load of downers, which I swallowed with Jack Daniels, only for it all to come up again about an hour later, pouring out of my nose like a horror film. I was new to all this stuff and you could say things were not really going very well. I kept on trying though.

The guy with the little house just loved to wind people up when they were stoned, as they often were round at his place, and I remember him chasing me up the little stairs with an axe, which in my state I was sure he was going to use. He didn't though of course and I almost saw the funny side, when I finally unlocked the bathroom door and came cautiously back downstairs to his roars of laughter, his girlfiend was always really nice to me though.

Not long after that, Andy moved out and got a flat with his mate, Pete, who looked like Johnny Rotten, on the rough estate at the edge of town. The walls were plastered with photo's and press cuttings of The Sex Pistols and it soon became the place to go on a Friday night, where about 8 or 9 of us would sit, listening to Lou Reed, The Doors, The Velvet Underground and various punk albums and see just how stoned we could get, which was usually very. We'd all chip in to go and buy an eighth or a quarter of dope and after the mandatory waiting around for the dealer to turn up, we'd make it last, using bongs that we made out of big plastic coke bottles and a biro, or sometimes doing hotknives or blowbacks, until we fell over.

Pete and Andy's flat, Lakes Estate, 1979

Occasionally someone would turn up with some speed, usually blues or dexy's, which always made the nights last longer. Later in the evenings, when we ran out of drink, we

Damaged Goods

used to draw lots for who was going to go to the pub under the flat before it closed and buy more beer.

It was rough, to put it mildly and was still populated by ageing Teds and others, who didn't like punks much, but usually we somehow got away with dirty looks and remarks, or the occasional shove in the back. Sometimes I'd stay the night on the floor, or if I wasn't too wrecked and didn't fancy waking up amongst the empty cans and full ashtrays, I'd walk the three miles home to the village. The funny thing is that I never used to get a hangover in those days and was always fine the day after.

Though I didn't get into any trouble at that last school, I only ended up staying there for 6 idle, wasted weeks. I guess I had decided it wasn't going to go anywhere and that finally, at 16, my school days were over. I didn't exactly feel elated, but it did feel inevitable. After telling my unimpressed parents what I was going to do, I decided to leave home and move into a bedsit in town, with my new found friends and at least I was doing something.

I was away from home at last. I never was going to live up to my parent's academic aspirations and by the time I moved out, my leaving was mutual.

I had a cramped little attic room in a guest house and was listening to Soft Cell singing 'Bedsitter' on my record player, which sat on the armchair. There wasn't room for anything else in there, so I had all my clothes and records on the floor, everything from Elvis to the Pistols, 25 years of Rock and Roll.

From Mum and Dad's six bedroom, 3 bathroom house to this and it didn't feel much like victory or freedom. My room was at the end of a narrow corridor, with a shared bathroom at the end, which had a cracked bath and leaky old taps. Sometimes on a Sunday, Dad would come round with a box full of food for me, which kept me going for a few days, but apart from that, bless him, I was on my own.

Damaged Goods

For me, being a punk was just an escape from myself and what I had or hadn't done. Like the mods did 20 years earlier, escaping the greyness of life by dressing up and pretending to be someone else, every day. Nothing to do with politics or drawing attention to myself, as I well knew that there were easier ways to get a smack in the mouth.

So, on with my Anarchy shirt and trousers and the new black Pixie boots that I'd pinched from outside a shop in Luton the week before. On with some black eyeliner and nail varnish and a bit of lipstick to finish. I always wore a silver safety pin through my ear to match the studded belt that my brother had given me.

Me in my Vivienne Westwood gear.

My friend Tony came up from his room downstairs to see if I wanted to eat with him before we went out. When I got down there he had the Ramones album 'It's Alive' playing. He always seemed to look after me, he was the local boxing champion, drummer in the top local punk band and leader of the town punks.

The week before, a couple of pissed up older blokes had dragged me down the alley as I came out of the pub at closing time. I had a good go but was no match for them really. They didn't like punks and were giving me a good kicking when Tony hurried up. He knocked them both over without a word, one punch each. Bang bang. The Stooges 'Search and Destroy' was drifting out of the side window at the time, it's one of those things you remember.

I had some of the vegetarian food he'd cooked, which was unusual in those days and off we went to the pub. We arrived to find all our friends were in there, as well as some of the Bedford and Luton punks and skinheads. There were studs, zips, safety pins, chains, torn shirts and multi coloured hair everywhere, as punk had not yet become the uniform of ripped jeans, leather jacket and mohican haircuts - you weren't supposed to all look the same. I had jet black hair and wore make up and a kilt and fishnets, with studded biker boots and a Vivienne Westwood parachute shirt.

Sometimes I was told that I looked more like a New Romantic, Marc Almond from Soft Cell or someone like that. I didn't know if that was supposed to be an insult and didn't care, they did a cover of a Northern Soul song and I thought they were great.. It was all dressing up to me.

I'd bumped into Steve Strange in the Vivienne Westwood shop last week, down the Kings Road in Chelsea. He said he had a band called Visage. I'd met him at a few gigs and stuff and he told me they were playing at the Blitz club, must go down to see that. I bought their single 'Fade to Grey' and I thought they were great.

The Clash were singing 'Clash City Rockers' on the jukebox. It was The Leighton Carnival and the local band I was in,

Damaged Goods

State of Shock, were playing at the Bossard Hall, backing up The Subhumans. What a buzz.

The band I was in with me on guitar, backing up The Subhumans

Being in that pub was like having our own little world, our own family. We all fitted in. We still got paid weekly in cash, but so did everyone then, that or the Dole, so we all spent the week waiting for Friday, the weekend was our life. Like the words to that song 'Monday I've Got Friday On My Mind.' We went to a different gig every week in those days and the list would be a long one; The Clash, The Jam, The Banshees, The Cure, The Undertones, Adam and The Ants, Stiff little Fingers, Madness and The Specials, to name a few.

The concert was excellent, with a good sound, from the Black Sheep Promotions P.A., and the crowd going crazy. The night seemed to last forever as I flailed away at my Rickenbacker copy guitar, trying to do a Pete Townsend. We got a great review in the fanzine the next month and it said I played a good guitar. Hmm. This was theatre and I loved it.. I ended up going home with a punk girl who had been staring at me the whole time I was playing, there were groupies, even on our small scale. It was very flattering and always nicer to wake up next to someone. Her mum even made us breakfast in the morning, as we lay in bed listening to Lou Reed's 'Rock and roll animal.' Now that's a good guitar.

Another weekend down at the Bossard Hall and it was Ian's 21st birthday. He had UKDecay from Luton playing, who were getting to be a real popular band with an LP and everything. It was packed solid and we were all down the front by the time the music started.

The singer, Abbo, had Tartan punk clothes and brothel creepers, with big backcombed hair. They started their song 'Middle of the road man,' Spon's crashing guitar was great. Tony was watching their drummer, Steve Harle and shadow boxing to the beat, they were his favourite band. They were very good. Abbo's a great front man, twirling his studded belt around above his head as the audience went mad. The music was putting the hairs up on the back of my neck as Ian got up on stage. Abbo had his arm round Ian's

Damaged Goods

shoulders. Singing 'Do you like Ian' to the chorus and everyone was cheering. What a great party.

Later on, after it had finished, I was walking home down Doggett Street when I saw two guys playing a Piano under a streetlight in the rain. They were laughing, pissed out of their heads. They wheeled it out of the hall after the gig and no one had said a word.

The following week I went over to Bedford to meet some friends and was sitting in the Cadena cafe in the arcade, drinking a pot of tea, minding my own business. I used to go up there to smoke when I was at school, which was only 4 years earlier, but already seemed a lifetime away.

On the next table sat a big meathead and his girlfriend and as I got up to leave he looked at me- 'You staring at my bird mate?'

'No.'

'Why, don't you fancy her then?'

'No.'

'What, are you saying she's ugly?'

'No.'

'You a queer then? You fuckin look like one'

'No.'

'So you do fancy her then'

'No I don't, leave me alone.'

I turned to go and he went to get up. Oh fuck, here we go then, now or never. I picked up the stool I had been sitting on and hit him with it three times as he came at me. He lay still on the floor, a little surprised, as his girlfriend screamed at me to leave him alone.

I was a thin effeminate looking 17 year old and he must have been 2 or 3 years older and 2 or 3 stone bigger than me. What was I supposed to do, let him hit me first and do me the damage?

I always hated bullies. I walked quickly back to the train station with my legs shaking, half expecting a gang of blokes to come after me at any moment. They didn't, but I wouldn't be going back to Bedford again in a hurry.

As it happened, the next time was the infamous riot at the Bunyan centre, when The Angelic Upstarts played, backed up by UK Decay. They had just started, doing their song 'Sexual,' when all of a sudden, a big skinhead got up on stage. Topless, with just his Sta- Prest and braces, he was covered in blood and screaming 'Seig Heil' The skins thought it was the punks but it wasn't, it was the bouncers. Too late though and we were so outnumbered.

Me and Tony stood back to back in the hall, punching every bone head that came our way. I was slapping them with my belt, but the fuckers wouldn't stay down. The hall was full of people fighting – fists, belts, and boots. They pulled Abbo off the stage and Spon was hitting skins with his guitar as a punk girl swung the mike stand, knocking them over like skittles. Fuckin 'ell!

Over by a fire exit one of the UKDecay road crew was getting a hiding from three skins. Me and Tony ran out and they ran off. Outside it was worse, with everyone fighting the coppers. One grabbed Tony from behind. I fired a left hook behind his ear and he went down. That's six years of kung fu for you. I'd been boxing with Tony a few times but it wasn't really my thing. Sometimes I ran through the woods and met up with him for a run round Stockgrove park.

The copper never saw me coming but his mate did though. Now he was coming at me with his truncheon when all of a sudden, the big skinhead from the stage grabbed hold of the copper, picked him up and threw him against the wall. He was trying to stop the skins from fighting the punks but it was too late. Police vans and cars were getting turned over, like the wild west or something.

Damaged Goods

We ran back to our van, with loads of other Leighton punks piling in. We could hear the dogs barking and I saw the skin being dragged off by 5 coppers, still trying to fight them. I guess he'd be receiving some special attention in the cells then.

We drove out very carefully and were waved out by a copper. John Peel was playing The Only Ones on the radio, 'Another Girl Another Planet,' then Spizz Energi's 'Where's Captain Kirk?.' Excellent. The riot was on Anglia news the next night and it blamed the punks and skins, we knew it was the bouncers though, never believe the media.

Next day, hungry and thirsty, I went into the cafe. Punky Suzy was working in there waitressing and she was beautiful. Like Diana Rigg in her younger days, but she had black & purple hair, with fishnets & safety pins and her waitress coat. That was it though, nothing else underneath, as I found out when she came round later. It didn't take long for us to get it off and our clothes were all over the place and we made a real mess of the bedroom, finally falling asleep listening to Iggy Pop's 'Turn Blue.' It felt like a night without end.

I bought a little Yamaha RS 100 motorbike. They weren't restricted in those days and it went well for its size. I took it up the village to show my biker friends and they just laughed. We all started out with a small one they said. Bet you've still got one I said, wagging my little finger at them. I think it was because they knew I was a Donna Summer fan that they didn't take me seriously, but why did we have to like just one sort of music? That's like being racist, or sexist, or something.

Just as The Pistols could put the hairs up on the back of my neck with one chord, Donna Summer could make me cry with one note. Her songs were sweeping, poetic operettas about the world she moved in. Complete stories, romances, life on the street. The same way that Tom Waits sang about the dangerous, underside of America that existed like the Twilight Zone. I put them all on the turntable and escaped to other worlds with them, like friends, or lovers. Somewhere over the rainbow.

There are two of me, so maybe I'm crazy, but I loved Punk and I always loved Disco too. Check out Madleen Kane's 'Cherie,' Dalida's 'Gigi in Paradisco' singles, or Boris Midney's 'Beautiful Bend' and 'Pinnochio' albums though, they are masterpieces. I also knew they were having a damn good time in their night clubs, ignoring the endless dole queues and dressing up in all those lovely sparkly clothes, partying like there was no tomorrow.

We dressed down and sang about No Future and it's taken me a while to see it as that 'Glass half empty / Glass half full' thing. Wish I'd thought of it then. Maybe I should have been a disco queen, but I didn't know any, I only knew Punks.

One Friday night, down town after the pub, me and a friend decided to go to visit his girlfriend in Hemel Hempstead. He didn't have a crash helmet but fuck it, after 5 pints who cares? About halfway there and whilst going through a little village, a cop car appeared. My little bike with 2 punks on it, all studs and with my friend's pink hair blowing in the wind was asking for trouble. It wasn't quick enough for a getaway either.

Damaged Goods

With the blue light flashing we pulled over and they asked if it was mine. I showed them my documents which were all ok and then they asked why the rear light didn't work. They also asked where my friend's crash helmet was. I was giggling and they asked me if I'd been drinking. Blow into this, it's one of the old type breathalysers just a tube of crystals. If it turned green I was fucked but I gave it a good blow anyway. They looked at it and after five minutes it still hadn't changed colour. They couldn't believe it and neither could I. Well you can't go to Hemel with him like that they said, or with no back light. Fine, I told them I'd push it back to town.

They didn't think we were funny but eventually they drove off. I pinned the tube to my jacket lapel with the big safety pin from my ear and we got back on and rode on. Ho ho ho, I wore that tube for weeks.

Me, far right, my jacket and some of the LU7 Punks, 1981

Punky Suzy, it went somewhere, but it went wrong... One word, Heroin. How corny and filthy that shit is.

I was falling asleep with a spliff and Pink Floyds 'The Wall' or The Banshees, or Steel Pulse, whatever. We snorted crap Sulphate whenever we could find it, but that was it. It was for fun or escape and we all did it. Who the fuck was interested in Heroin? Not me.

I tried to love that girl, the way only teenagers can. You know when you see someone for the first time and they take your breath away? She was that stunning, every time I looked at her, with legs up to her ears. Everyone fancied her but it took me six months to realise she felt the same way about me.

That day in the cafe, I asked her round for a cup of tea when she finished work and she came. We fell on each other, I remember. I almost wish I didn't, but we had such a time.

She entered the local beauty contest and blimey she looked good. They were playing Heaven 17's 'Fascist Groove Thang.' The judges obviously didn't care for punks, or her outspokenness against general apathy. I think they preferred someone who dressed like a disco dolly & wanted to help sick animals, well, that's who won anyway. You could see that the males in the audience had not been the ones who voted, only with their eyes.

I was proud to walk out of there with her but something was eating away at her. I asked the question and she lied and I knew she was lying.

Sometimes we'd go out in the morning, just as it was getting light, after being up all night speeding, listening to The Buzzcocks, The Undertones, Sam and Dave, or Arthur Lee and Love. I always thought that their track '7 & 7 is' was the first Punk record, not Lou Reed or MC5.

We'd wait for the milkman and then we'd pinch milk and orange juice from peoples doorsteps, sometimes we'd get bread too. Obvious in our bondage trousers and coloured hair, creeping through the early morning mist. At night

Damaged Goods

we'd go to the Chinese Takeaway at closing time and they'd give us whatever they hadn't sold to eat.

One night, outside, there was some older guy.

'What the fuck do you look like?' he said.

I could see his point - Kilt, fishnets & biker boots, Destroy shirt, Black & orange hair and makeup, and that was just me!

'I hate bikers' he said, I said I wasn't one and he said he hated queers as well. I said I wasn't one of those either and bang! I landed him my best shot on the chin.

He didn't go down though, he launched at me with both fists flying. There we were dancing around, throwing drunken combinations at each other, when suddenly the Chinese guy from the chippie ran out. He had some Nunchakas and his friend had got a big fish knife. Uh-Oh!

Suzy jumped on the guys back, gouging at his eyes, whilst I had one eye I couldn't see out of and blood pouring from my nose. At last I got him right on the temple and he was down. Suzy got off and he looked worse than I did.

The Chinese guys were laughing and patting me on the back, but I watched as the guy got to his feet. That's some punch he said, but you still look like a c**t. Fair enough. 'Wanker' said Suzy and off he went.

We got loads of food that night and ended up in the churchyard, having sex on top of an old tomb, which made me think of all those girls in the old Hammer horror films. Mmmm. Very gothic, or an omen.

It was winter and it'd been snowing for four days, with two inches of hard packed snow and ice on the roads. I decided to go and visit some friends on my bike and got a few miles out of the village, when the throttle cable snapped, leaving me stranded. No way I could push it in that so I walked to the nearest village phone box and rang my mate John. He laughed and said he'd be there in half an hour, so I sat there, shivering and smoking. When he finally turned up he wasn't in his Mum's car, he was on his bike with a tow rope wrapped round his waist.

We had a look at the offending cable to see if it could be bodged, but it'd snapped off just where it goes into the engine casing and was beyond repair. Right then he said, I'll tow you. I thought it wouldn't be as easy as it used to be, getting a tow through the woods from school, on my mates FS1e. But anyway, we tied the rope around his rear grab rail and my front forks and moved off, slowly. We took the back roads through the woods and kept having to stop, as with one pair of gauntlets between us, my hand was hurting from the cold.

It got a bit tricky going up steep hills, sliding across the road like a pendulum and with not much grip on the snow, I had both my feet down, boots scraping along the snow. When we finally made it back, I couldn't move my right hand, it was frozen solid. We didn't see one car either, not surprised really, you'd have to be mad to go out in that.

Fuck my hand hurt as it warmed up, but I got the bike fixed at Sid Mularney's bike shop the next week.

On the way to work at my Dad's factory one day, I was overtaking a Vauxhall Viva and just as I got alongside, it turned in front of me. Smack! straight into the back wing. I flew over the car and landed flat on my back on the verge.

I got up. I was feeling dazed and I couldn't see my bike, where the fuck had that gone? The driver came up and said he didn't see me.

Damaged Goods

'Where's my bike?' I kept saying. After a few minutes I saw it, it had slid round the corner, into the entrance to Lancer Boss. I walked over and picked it up for an inspection. It had a broken clutch lever, broken indicator and a bent footrest and that was it. The car driver said I was lucky and he was right.

After exchanging insurance details I got back on and rode it the rest of the way to work, stuck in first gear.

I sat in the canteen for a while, having a cup of tea before going into work, feeling a bit shaky. The bike went back into Sid Mularney's shop to be fixed again and I went to the doctor and got some cortisone injections in my shoulder, which has never been right since. Bikes eh?

A month or so later, me and John got invited to a party by my friend Pigsy. Don't know how he got invited, but it was being held at a sort of approved school in a Georgian country house, with a lake and everything.

Me and John went on our bikes and Pigsy turned up in his M.G. Midget. There were loads of people there and loads of drink and we'd bought a big lump of blow with us. To start with we hid in Pigsy's car to skin up as we didn't really know anybody there. John could skin up with his eyes closed and after a while the smell must have drifted up to the main lawn. It wasn't long before there were loads of people all smoking with us and we started to get on just fine.

Down by the lake there was a little boat chained up to the jetty. Someone got a key and unlocked the padlock and there we all were, out on the lake stoned out of our heads, drinking wine, at borstal! Ho ho ho!

John was working like a man possessed and just kept passing spliffs out, like a production line, until finally we were so wasted that we decided to get on our bikes and go home. Pigsy said he wasn't fit to drive and he was gonna sleep in his car, which he couldn't even get out of by then, he was just a giggling mess. We couldn't sleep on our bikes though, so off we went, weaving up the long driveway.

We stuck very close to each other, trying to ride carefully through the country lanes, when suddenly there was a big white blur, like a flash, right in my face. What was that!? I was doing 50 miles an hour and I slammed on the brakes and skidded to a stop.

John pulled up next to me and we both pulled off our crash helmets. His face looked as white as mine. Fuckin' ell he said. Did you see that? I wasn't sure what I'd seen, I was so wrecked. What the fuck was it? Was I seeing things?

He said that I was just dive bombed by a great white owl, that almost flew right into me. I guess it must have been my headlight, but it wasn't what you needed when you were stoned. It did kind of sober me up though, for the rest of the way home. Have to watch out for those killer owls man, they're everywhere! Cheech and Chong anyone?

Another night, after a UKDecay gig in Luton, I came back late. I walked into the flat and there was Suzy and a few friends of ours. She hadn't come to the gig and had said she wasn't well.

The Velvet Underground were singing 'Venus in Furs' but there was something else too. 'What the fuck is that?' Spoons with lighters underneath and syringes. Fuck. I might have been naive but I sure wasn't stupid. She had a dog lead round her arm. Fuck. 'Get that shit out of my house.'

Click. All of a sudden her new friends made sense, her colds made sense, her complexion and her distance made sense. She was right, she wasn't well. She lied again and again I knew she was lying. I told the others to fuck off and she said she was sorry. She said she'd stop, she said she loved me more. I cried as I held her and I asked her why she didn't stop. She couldn't tell me what was so bad in her past to need that much escape.

Damaged Goods

We split up and it hurt. It wasn't meant to end like that and I felt lost. Was it someone's fault? I found her dealer. I knew him, he knew me. My head went and I kicked in his door, I broke his nose, I broke his wrist and I cracked some ribs. I trashed his flat as he watched and told him if I had to come back I would kill him. I wasn't lying, I conferred with my friend John - Boot of the car, tarpaulin, quicksand down the woods.

Eventually her dealer got busted and went to prison, maybe just as well, but she found another. It was like a plague had come to town, I thought that the needle marks looked like vampire bites, sucking the life out of the town's young. English Gothic, at its darkest and suddenly it seemed like everyone was on it.

Me and Suzy finished for good and the people around us were changing too. Punk was dying on its feet and even the New Romantics were finished.

That's it then, playtime over, no more dressing up. I cut off my dyed hair, sold my Punk clothes and left town.

A good thing about being a villager was that I wasn't stuck there, fuck that. Suzy's parents knew and they sent her to Rehab in the country somewhere and that was the end of punk for me.

There's a verse from Edgar Allen Poe's 'Alone' which kept going around in my head which I reckon about wrapped it up…….

I moved back into Mum and Dad's and tried to settle back into village life with my old friends. We had a good night at the Christmas Disco, which was now held in the new Cricket Club, getting drunk and dancing. Everyone was there, Mr Steve and Uncle Malc, Jam, John and Pigsy and all the old lot. I didn't feel I fitted any more though.

After a few months I met a girl from the new city at another disco, who I started going out with. I guess I was trying to live out some clean living fantasy of what might have been and tried to make her Suzy, she wasn't though, of course and it wasn't her fault.

Two passionate years we lasted, I got on well with all her family and lost myself in their lives, I even went on a family holiday with them to Spain. We talked about getting engaged and stuff, but when it came to it, I guess the glitter had worn off a bit and my heart just wasn't in it anymore. It broke her heart when I finished with her and I wasn't very proud of myself, hurting someone who loved me like that, but I couldn't lie to her, not when our lives were at stake.

A few weeks later I went back to Leighton and tracked Suzy down... I saw her, I still wanted her, but it wasn't her any more. She looked the same, but she looked different. She had wrinkles round her sunken eyes and seemed to cry a lot. I guess she realised that she'd shot her innocence into her veins and pissed it all away. What a waste. It was like there was someone else living in her body. She'd haunted me, but I said good bye, again.

I had given up all my punk friends when I left town, I couldn't face them. That whole place just reminded me of Suzy and punk and there were too many people getting hurt around me, myself included and I needed to do something different to change that.

Damaged Goods

I joined the new local Martial Arts Academy and started going 2 nights a week and every Sunday afternoon. We did hands, feet and weapons and I loved all of it. Our instructor always had a ghetto blaster on during the warm up sessions and within a couple of months, I could do sets of 150 sit ups, squat thrusts, leg raises and all the other stuff, without any trouble and loved the full contact sparring sessions. I also learnt to hate the track 'Footloose,' from the film of the same name, which he played endlessly every week as well.

It's funny how, over the years, certain pieces of music from films stick in your mind. Some of the ones that still go around in my head are from going to the cinema and some from watching videos at home. For me there's 'Lara's Theme' from Dr Zhivago, the theme from 'Jaws,' The James Bond Theme, 'The Godfather Waltz' and 'Amapola' from 'Once Upon a Time in America.'

All sorts of songs from Musicals are in there too, like Fiddler on the Roof, South Pacific, West Side Story, The Sound of Music and Chitty Bang Bang. They sort of become part of your own soundtrack in the end.

I sold the little 100 to a friend and bought a Suzuki GT380 two stroke triple. That was a nice noise, I could just sit and listen to it ticking over, a lovely uneven three cylinder burble and it roared well at the red line too.

My Suzuki GT 380, outside Pigsy's

One night after the pub, me and the village bikers decided to go up to London to see my hippie cousin, the one who'd left his Joan Baez record at my Dad's house all those years ago. After all screaming up the M1, racing each other, we sat and smoked dope and dried Flyagaric mushrooms for a couple of hours. Bloody hell! That was some buzz!

About two in the morning we left and were just getting the ton up past Scratchwood services, when Bang! My bike started to wobble furiously and then the back wheel locked up. I held on for my life.

They say things go in slow motion at times like that, but not for me it didn't. It skidded to a stop, with the sound of screaming rubber, in a dead straight line right onto the hard shoulder. I couldn't believe my fuckin' luck.

I got off, shakily, to assess the damage. The chain had snapped and wrapped itself around the back wheel. How the fuck did I survive that? My mates came back in a minute or so, as the Motorway was empty in those days. They looked and they couldn't believe my luck either. I didn't think I was gonna get too many chances like that. We were staring in disbelief at the dead straight black skid mark, stretching back up the road. I sat and shakily fumbled a cigarette out of my pack and had a smoke, whilst my mates went off to get a pick up.

I sat there alone for half an hour, watching my hands shaking, until they came back in an open Land Rover, with some ramps.

'I think that's it for me and bikes' I said. They didn't say anything. Home.

Damaged Goods

I went to see U2 play The Milton Keynes Bowl with the bikers and my brother came down from London too, with all his footballing mates. REM, The Ramones and Spear of Destiny were the support bands and they all played real good. The Ramones seemed to play the entire 'It's Alive' LP as the rain came down in sheets, which looked excellent.

But... During a lull in the rain, one of my brothers mates, Brad, got down from the bank and started singing. 'Blue Heaven.' It's one they sang on the terraces at Arsenal. All the rest sang along, repeating every line until, after two renditions he finished.

Half the Mk Bowl was applauding, cheering for more, so he sang it again. Seemed like the whole place was singing along –

'Just Molly and me,' (just molly and me)

'And Baby Makes Three' (and baby makes three)

'Living in my' (living in my),

'Blue heaven' (blue heaven).

The audience erupted, what a star. He took a bow to more cheering. That was almost better than any of the bands I thought and I don't think I was the only one.

Shortly after that my brother moved to The States, to be a soccer coach in Atlanta. I wondered if he'd teach them how to fight on the terraces.

I started to go around with some of my brother's old mates, from the next town. These were different - graduates mostly, who had decided to take more than just the one year off. They were having a damn good time too it seemed to me.

There was Fruit (who wasn't), Junior, Egg, Fatman (who wasn't) Silver Fox, and my old friends Storky and Pigsy, as well as a host of others.

'Have you ever been to Glastonbury?' they asked,

'No' I said, 'Isn't that just for bikers?' 'We're going, why don't you come with us?' they said. Oh yes!

We drove down at four in the morning in Storky's Vauxhall Viva, smoking joints and listening to Roxy Music singing 'Like a Hurricane' along with the rest of their live album and The Shaggs singing 'My Pal Foot Foot' on his cassette player - What the fuck is that? It was so bad it was brilliant! I don't remember much else of that journey. I wasn't used to smoking that much. We were followed by their friends Robin in his newly restored MG roadster, Scum on his big Suzuki and Pigsy, on his yellow Honda 400 four.

I don't remember how everyone else got there, but finally we arrived and fuck me, it was like something out of Mad Max. There were Hell's Angels and other assorted biker gangs, Hippies and Students. This was before the giant fences and before police were on site, they had an agreement that they'd just sit outside the entrance unless there was trouble. There wasn't any while we were there, not really.

Though there were only about 35,000 people there in those days, I had never seen that many people in one place for a party. I could not believe this could exist in England.

There were people walking around with satchels, shouting out 'Red Leb 15 a quarter, Whizz 10 pound a gram' over and over. Like market traders. The market. Bloody Hell!

There were stalls for everything. Big blackboards with lists of what they were selling. You have got to be fuckin' kidding, it was all drugs!

White lightning £2.50. Samurai blotters £2.50. Red Leb £15 1/4. Black £20. Speed (good stuff) £10. It was everywhere you looked. They would sell you cans of beer as well and we were like kids in a sweetshop.

We bought some Red Leb and asked a biker what the white lightning things were. He laughed, 'it's acid' he said, 'LSD. Where have you been hiding?'

Damaged Goods

'Not at University' I said and I started to feel that maybe I had missed out on something.

I had never seen it before. I asked if they were any good and he asked if we'd ever done it before.

'Yes!' we all said.

'These babies last a whole day' he said, 'Are you sure you want them?'

'You bet your sweet bippy' we all said.

He laughed and handed us a small square of blotting paper each, with a Japanese letter on them.

Here we go then, I was nervous and excited, I couldn't fuckin' wait. I thought this stuff had disappeared, It was like a legend. Half an hour later and nothing. Hmm I thought We'd been ripped off.

We were sitting under a pylon on the hillside and there was someone playing with a sort of white bird thing that they were throwing to each other, like a paper plane. I was watching it glide between them and it looked so beautiful. I turned to Storky and he was watching it too.

'Isn't that beautiful?' I said and suddenly I felt very strange, like I was talking in slow motion. Everything felt so spacious.

'Bloody 'ell' said Storky.

'Fuck's sake' said Junior and Scum was just grinning from ear to ear.

It felt like sitting in a strong wind, without the wind. 'It's life you're feeling' said Storky. Wow! He was right. That's exactly what it was, life coursing through me. It was everywhere - I could see it in the air, in the grass, even in the clouds. Those clouds, they were white and fluffy and I could see one that looked like a lamb. It was jumping around the sky and I was laughing, laying on my back and I felt like I was in a film set.

Nothing felt real, like special effects, everything had changed and I felt like I was seeing the world for the first time. It was so wonderful. I said I couldn't speak. Storky laughed. Yes you can he said, but I couldn't quite understand how I was doing it.

I was losing my powers of conscious movement, looking at my hands without quite remembering what they were.

'Come on' said Fruit, 'let's go for a walk.'

We all looked at him like he was mad, then we all got up and followed him.

It was like my body was on automatic. My head felt wide open and cool.

'Hey Storky' I said. 'I can't, I can't' I couldn't manage to say any more than that. He patted me on the back and told me I'd be alright and off we went. Snow white and the seven dwarves.

It felt like we were in a cartoon. There was a beautiful Hari Krishna girl trying to get Pigsy to say Krishna.

'How about a blowjob?' he said.

They just kept repeating the same things. I thought he should leave her alone, she thought he should say Krishna, he thought she should give him a blowjob. It all seemed very complicated to me.

Everyone began to look weird as we walked past them. There was another Krishna girl who looked awful familiar. I stared at her for a while and she smiled back at me, click - It's Poly Styrene, the singer from Xray Spex.

'Aren't you Poly Styrene?' I asked her.

'I used to be' she said and laughed.

Blimey, Vive le Punk!

It finally occurred to me that everyone else in the place was out of their heads too and that seemed like a good thought.

Damaged Goods

My stomach was butterflies and my eyes were... I don't know what they were.

Seeing, breathing, walking, it all seemed so miraculous. I finally saw how wonderful life really was and how small a part we play in this world. It seemed like the world loved us all.

'Yes' said Storky, 'it does, we are its children.'

Did I say that out loud?

'I don't know' said Storky, 'but I heard you somehow.'

'Fuck me!' I thought, 'What is this stuff, a present from God or something?'

I felt like I was floating. I don't know how long we wandered around the site until eventually we got back to our tents. Robin wasn't with us anymore. He had his girlfriend with him. We knew he'd be ok, but his car was still here, parked next to us. Uh-Oh.

Fruit said 'wouldn't it be funny if we hid his car?'

'Don't you think he might get upset?' I said.

'Oooh no' said Fruit.

We were starting to get the hang of this stuff. About five minutes and he had managed to find a key to open both the door and the Crooklok from somewhere. He started it up and drove it slowly about 100 yards and parked it behind some other tents. It now seemed hilarious and we were all giggling.

'Let's go and watch a band' said Junior.

Blimey, I'd forgotten about the bands. We got down to the main stage and Black Uhuru were just starting to play. We were sitting on the grass at the back of the crowd. Bloody hell they were heavy and they were very good. I had never seen a reggae band before, wow!

We noticed that Pigsy was looking increasingly strange, even to us. It was very hot and sunny and I turned to Pigsy, telling him I was so hot I could just about peel my skin off. It was supposed to be funny but he didn't think so. He gibbered something unintelligible, then he got up and ran off into the crowd. Everyone else was howling with laughter.

'Quick!' said Fruit, 'Run the other way!' and that's what we did, all laughing, It felt like hide and seek.

I couldn't quite seem to remember what my watch was supposed to tell me. I was looking at it and it meant nothing. I asked Egg what it was for and he dissolved into a helpless fit of giggles, doubled up on the grass. After a while I thought 'Who cares?' Not me. Then Egg got up and pissed on Fruits legs, just like that. He was laughing out loud now and so were we, but not Fruit. But Egg was one big muscle-bound thug and Fruit wasn't.

I don't know what bands we saw after that. We made our way back up the hill and found another Hari Krishna tent. We went in to find it was a free food tent. Oh yeah, I'd forgotten about eating. We got some food and it tasted real good. We were still completely off our trolleys.

'Get a chair' said junior,

'What for?' I asked.

'We'll have a bonfire' he said.

I said that we couldn't do that, but he just replied 'Oh yes we can, just take one.'

They were folding wooden ones and I took one, as we all did. The Hari Krishna's just smiled at us. What the fuck was going on?

'Glastonbury' said Fatman, 'It's great isn't it?'

Yeah, it sure was. Back by the tents the bonfire looked great. We were drinking Scrumpy and staring into the flames, smoking some Rocky Gold.

Damaged Goods

Robin found his car and drove home with the hump as he didn't think it was very funny, but that made it even funnier to us. We laughed at him as he drove off, tripping, all the way back to M.K. in the dark, blimey!

Glastonbury, 1983

Much later, a figure came stumbling into the firelight, sweating, with a face of fear and he was crying. It was Pigsy. He'd been gone hours. He sat down in the fire sobbing until we pulled him out. I'm not sure how many hours passed but he finally managed to speak.

He said he fell over down near the front of the crowd and when he looked up he saw three giant Rastas staring down at him.

He said they were a hundred foot tall. He Freaked. Then he took off and flew up into the sky he said. He looked down from on high and shouted at himself to run away and just kept shouting it. Eventually the giants left him alone and he dropped down and fell into a yellow sea. He was drowning in it, trying to swim, when someone had picked him up. It wasn't a yellow sea after all, it was his biker jacket, yellow to match his Bike.

Poor Pigsy, he didn't seem to be coping with it all very well, or having a good time, like we all were.

What seemed like weeks later I was leaning against Storky's car. I was unable to string a sentence together but I wished that I could.

'When's this stuff going to stop?' I finally managed to ask, fuckin' ell, It'd been 14 hours. All I remember about the rest of the weekend is smoking dope, seeing 'The Funboy Three' doing the Doors song 'The End,' with Terry Hall waving a flaming American flag whilst singing it in the dark. Wow man...

Damaged Goods

Dad had just got me my first car, after selling the Suzuki, it was a 1976 green golf 1600ls. No more bikes for me.

My first car!

We all piled in at midnight and drove down to town to the nearest nightclub. I'd never been in one before as an adult, as being a punk meant it wasn't a good idea. Still, I wasn't a punk anymore and this felt better, not standing out.

Emma the beautiful disco dolly from the village came along too. We got to the club and went straight up to the bar and after a few pints we were all dancing to Lulu singing 'Shout.' This place wasn't exactly classy.

Suddenly it was half two in the morning. Unfortunately Emma had gone off with someone else, not me, and it was time to go home. We all crammed into the car just as a police van and a squad car cruised past, down to the club entrance. Bollocks. With pissed up logic, I decided to go over the curb at the edge of the car park and straight onto the road, instead of going past the coppers.

Halfway over and the exhaust caught on the curb, as there were a few too many people in it. Oh shit, it now sounded like a tractor and all my mates got out and ran off.

Nothing else for it I decided and got out and crawled underneath, trying to put the concertina section back into the pipe where it had been ripped it out. I must have been pissed. I couldn't believe it when it went straight back in, but just as I finished I saw a big pair of boots walking along the car. They stopped right next to me.

A voice said 'Ello Ello, What's going on 'ere then?' Oh fuck. That's all I needed, a copper with a sense of humour. As it turned out, it was. I slid out from under the car and looked up into the face of my old childhood friend Geoff.

'Fuck me!' I said, 'You're a copper.'

'Fuck me!' he said, 'You're pissed.'

Yes. I'm afraid I was.

I told him what happened and he asked who it was that ran off. I told him they were the village lot.

'Some mates!' he said.

Hmm. He asked if I could drive straight. I seemed to have sobered up a bit and said yes, I thought so.

'Hang on here then' he said.

He walked back across the car park to where the rest of the coppers were and had a word. Then he came back over and told me to get down onto the road and follow him, said he'd take me out to the village turn.

He pulled round in front of me and stuck his blue flashing light on. He was laughing. Fuck me, I couldn't believe my luck! I followed him out of town and we saw my mates from the village walking home. Me and Geoff both beeped our horns and stuck our fingers up at them as we passed, he even put his siren on, that made them jump! They didn't know what was happening. Fuck 'em they could walk. Teach them to run off.

I got to the village turn and Geoff stopped and got out. He came over and asked if I'd be alright going up the lane.

Damaged Goods

'Yes' I said.

'Good, don't do it again then' he said.

'Message received and understood captain' I said.

He told me to fuck off, laughing. It's what we used to say to each other when we used to play 'Star Trek.'

'Thanks Geoff,' I said, 'I am such a fuckin idiot.'

'Yep,' he said – 'Ain't we all.'

He got in his squad car and drove off back into town. I drove home, carefully, up to the safety of the village and bed. Could have been worse, could've been a cell.

I thought about it and I signed up for 6th Form College as a mature student. What me? You've got to be having a laugh.

But off I went and after a few weeks I made some new friends. What a bunch! There was Dj Picci, Gordon, Dylan and Jo Bombshell, Funky Colin and Daz, and Matty and Hann. Blimey she was a babe. Loads of others too, all into music. We went to see Cabaret Voltaire. They were having fun and I needed it.

Sixth form was just like school though, with tossers telling me what to do. Fuck 'em, what did they know? They'd never left school. How butch, rebel without a brain me.

I met this French guy Francis, from Bordeaux. He was an assistant teacher, over here for a year or so. He was into music and we got on great. He was lodging with another teacher who seemed to have loads of cats and her house stank. We all went around together. Some of them knew Storky and co. What a gang. They had a group, Ha Ha Guru, who were a sort of cross between Psychedelic Small Faces and Japan. Fruit sang the Dave Sylvain vocals whilst Storky did the cheeky chappie stuff and Fatman played the keyboards.

They played at the Joint and they were great and very Avant Garde. They were more of a studio band really though, as that's where Storky worked and he had access to all the studio toys, so their tapes were great - Flugal horns, bongos and echoing guitars, real trippy stuff. Fancy that!

Ha Ha Guru, playing at The Joint, MK

Damaged Goods

A couple of months later me and Storky got some acid, Pink Panthers. We went out in my car to a pub in town. The trip came on in the pub.

'This is too much' I said and it was.

'Alright' he said and out we went to the car.

'Storky,' I said, 'I can't drive.'

'Yeah you can, just sit here for a few minutes.'

I wasn't sure if I was dreaming, it wasn't that strong but it was a job to think properly.

I put on the cassette player and it was Mike Bloomfield, Steve Stills and Al Kooper's 'Super Session' L.P. Oh for fuck's sake, that guitar! Storky was laughing and so was I. A friend of mine had bought me that L.P. for my 9th Birthday, a lifetime ago. I didn't like it then, as it wasn't Slade or T.Rex, but I sure liked it now.

The tape I'd made for the car must have been full of crackles and hisses, but I didn't notice any that night. The trip was coming on with a vengeance now and I opened my door and sat with my legs out in the car park. The car stereo sounded like nothing I'd ever heard, how could it sound like that? It was only two tinny little door speakers. Storky said that it was fuckin' incredible and he was right, it was.

We sat there listening until the tape stopped after 45 long minutes. Wow, that was definitely some guitar.

'Let's go to a gig' said Storky.

OK and suddenly I was driving and everything seemed slowww. I looked from the speedo to the mirror, mirror to the speedo and oooh yes, I mustn't forget the road as well.

Slight paranoia started to creep in and then, Fuck! There's a police car coming the other way!

'It's ok' said Storky, 'You're doing fine. They don't know you're tripping.'

Oh bloody hell, of course they didn't! Mellow out man. I started to giggle. My car felt like a cartoon car. I knew that if we crashed it'd hurt though. I was being careful, but it was like steering a sail boat, which I hadn't done for a long time.

We got to the gig somehow and It was upstairs in a pub. Storky asked if I could play and I said that Yeah course I could, so up we got. Storky started a 12 bar on the keyboard and I'm stood there with the guitar, just looking at it. Oh shit, what is this thing? I could not remember a single note.

People started to look at me expectantly- Uh-oh. Then, fuck me, the lights all went out. What's going on?

Storky was laughing and I thought I could see in the dark.

'It's a power cut' he said,

'Thank fuck for that. I'm sorry I just couldn't remember how to play.'

'Don't worry' he said, 'You were great!'

People were lighting candles as we went downstairs into the pub. Everywhere was now lit with candles and it looked like the olden days.

There were people I knew in there and they started trying to speak to me, but I couldn't speak. This was too much. We had a quick drink and made an exit. I cannot remember where we went after that, or where I woke up.

Some weeks later, Storky said there was an all night horror thing at Bletchley Cinema. Oh Goody, Acid and Nightmare on Elm Street and The Exorcist. Don't remember what the other ones were. My little sister came too as I think she liked one of Storky's friends. The Exorcist didn't seem scary like it had the first time I had seen it, years ago and we all spent the night giggling, but my little sister didn't know

Damaged Goods

what was going on. I couldn't exactly tell her we were tripping and by the end of the night we were tired out from laughing so much and she was terrified.

'Didn't you think they were scary?' she said.

No, we thought they were hilarious!

Oh dear, not a good example.

'Have you read Carlos Castaneda?' asked Storky 'Or Tom Woolf's Electric Kool Aid Acid Test, or Jay Stevens Storming Heaven?'

I hadn't and he gave me them. I read them over and over. I knew there was more to life and here it all was in print. After that, on week nights I was lost in the Mexican desert and sixties California. I was hooked.

Me and Francis got a flat at the YMCA in Milton Keynes. My old friend Mark the DJ helped me move in with his van and it took all day. It was 7 in the evening by the time we finished, though I didn't have that much stuff, just clothes and records and stuff.

We'd been there three days when someone knocked at the door. It was two girls, one had black and white dyed hair like a New Romantic and all they were wearing were baby doll nighties and furry kitten heel slippers and feather boas. Honestly!

They had a bottle of champagne and said they were our welcoming committee. Blimey. Francis had The Sisters of Mercy playing on the stereo and we sat and smoked red leb and drank the champagne and then we went to bed and were shagged stupid. So this was Milton Keynes. It was great; it was mad!

A night out at 'The Joint' club, with my friends Douggie and Neeta. All the college lot were there and Storky and co and Tony. It was new romantic crossed with punk and very trendy. Alien Sex Fiend were playing a concert and I thought that they looked like the New York Dolls a bit.

We were all speeding off our heads on Pink Novocaine. It was clean, not like Sulphate. We'd got it from our Scouse friend and it was heaven, he got good stuff. Two a.m. and the club shut. We went for a drive in Douggies Lotus, a 1969 Elan convertible, it was beautiful and it should've been. He'd just finished a nut & bolt restoration which I'd helped with, painted blue over white, with a gold stripe.

It was a warm summer night and cruising down the dual carriageway we saw something in the lights. What the fuck was that? It was a naked man, thumbing a lift! It was one of the transvestites from the club, he was six feet plus and looked like Pete Burns and was naked except for his black stiletto boots. We stopped. He was off his head on something but said he wasn't scared, he was just trying to pick up a man.

Damaged Goods

We left him laughing at the road side, as other cars sped past, beeping their horns. When we saw him at the Joint the next week, he said he'd pulled a really nice builder in the end.

This place really was crazy and I loved it.

Back to the flat and as I put my key in the lock, Bernard opened the door. He was a friend of Francis.' He was staying with us for a bit as he'd just come out of Jail in France, for armed robbery. His passport didn't say Bernard though. He could get them and they were very good.

He was covered in blood. Fuck. Where's Francis?

'Don't go in the kitchen' said Bernard, 'Francis is in there.'

I saw blood on the floor. Fuck. I went in the kitchen and there was blood on the walls, it was everywhere. Fuck. Francis was leaning over the sink. Fuck. He turned around and I saw it.

It was a fuckin' stag, a whole one! I couldn't believe it!

They'd been to a concert and they'd hit it driving back through the woods and brought it home, tied across the top of his Renault 5, like in The Deer Hunter. They hadn't seen any coppers they said and laughed as Bernard butchered it in our kitchen and he seemed to know what he was doing. Johnny Thunders was singing 'You can't put your arms around a Memory' whilst he did it.

For a week or two after that we ate venison, the food of kings. The communal bin cupboard was under the flats and they put the remains in there. There were two black bin bags full and one of them had the pair of antlers sticking out of the top. They stayed there for six days until the bin men took them and no one said a word. Yep, this place was crazy.

Fruit, Storky, Junior, Egg and me went on a day out, boating on the river in Cambridge, stoned out of our heads.

It was a job to get Fruit up in the daytime, as he usually drank special brew until he couldn't speak most nights, then went to bed with a sock tied round his eyes and cotton wool in his ears. I never liked getting that drunk myself, but each to his own.

His Mum was a nurse and despaired at him I think, berating him as he stumbled out through the house, but we all thought it was funny. We managed to get him up that morning though and all bundled into mine and Storky's cars for the drive.

We went straight to the river when we got there, hiring a couple of punts and loading them up with Red Stripe and some more Special Brew for Fruit. We glided along, going under chains and into people's private gardens, floating past them as they picnicked on their lovely riverside lawns, feeling like pirates.

Fruit, Archie and me, punting in Cambridge.

Damaged Goods

Later on we went to eat in a Jamaican restaurant, run by some hippies in the back room of a shop. They were great cooks and played Scientist and other Dub stuff as we sat and drank and smoked dope, until the food was ready. It had giant paper globe lampshades hanging from the ceiling that I found very interesting for some strange reason and I sat and stared at as my food got cold, until I got the munchies. It didn't matter as no one was in any hurry, just as well really. I don't remember the journey home at all, strangely enough.

There were plenty of other outings with that lot, Egg beating up 4 guys outside a nightclub on his own, for taking the mickey out of Fruit's hair, having a competition to see how much food we could eat in the local Indian restaurant, then trying to fill up the glass shades on the table with the left overs, all sorts of naughtiness really.

There were a lot of Characters where they lived. Crazy May and Mad Alec, the old couple who lived next door, used to take his Mum's little dog for walks and kept a diary of what sort of bowel movements it had.

There was their friend Drone's Dad down the road, who had a shed at the bottom of his garden full of old radio parts, where he used to sit and get drunk at night and talk to Mars, over the microphone. None of the radio parts were even connected, but we could hear him from behind the fence, talking loudly in his drunken Northern drawl –'Earth to planet Mars, Come in!' over and over again, for hours.

Their own Dad was just as bad, he had fought in the war and had medals to prove it, but his patriotism had long since been twisted by the whisky he drank. He used to keep half a pool cue by his armchair and every time a Jewish name appeared on the screen, he would beat the TV with it, shouting obscenities.

One time, he did it whilst I was there and Junior objected. A full on fight ensued, which ended when Junior had his Dad pinned to the floor, punching him and his Mum ran in with a cast iron saucepan and proceeded to hit her husband round the head, as Junior knelt on his arms. It might sound a bit dramatic, but I don't think I'd ever laughed as much as I did with that lot. Blimey, we had some fun.

Damaged Goods

Another night, I got back to the flat about 1 in the morning and I could hear Francis' stereo from his room, but I was knackered, so just went in and went to bed. Just as I was drifting off I heard a couple of almighty bangs and the front door flew open, then slammed closed again. I could hear a load of blokes shouting out on the landing and I realised they must have kicked it in. Fuck. Not that I had much, but if they came in they'd trash the place.

So, I picked up a heavy old motorbike chain that I had, pulled on my jeans and went to the door. I could still hear them outside, so I took a deep breath and threw the door open, jumping out, shouting 'Right, who kicked my fuckin' door in then?' It went quiet. I looked around and there were about 20 blokes stood there. Ooops!

'We're looking for the French bloke' one of them said.

Oh dear, what had he done? Probably upset them in the pub I guessed, but there was no time for diplomacy and it wouldn't take long to lose my element of surprise.

I shouted at them that he wasn't there and lunged at the nearest one.

'Whoa' he said, jumping backwards, 'Sorry mate, must have got the wrong flat'

I told them to fuck off and they all backed slowly across the landing, as I went quickly back in and slammed the door, before they got brave. I was shaking a bit to be honest and thought I might have been a bit over the top and certainly stupid, but what do you do? The next day Francis said he never even heard it all!

They must have found out later that it was the right flat, but they never came back, luckily for me.

They probably thought there was some nutter living there.

Bernard finally went home after a couple of months and Francis moved back to France at the end of the year. I was sorry to see him go, it had been great and I'd made a good friend there. He had a good leaving party though, with people shagging in the bath and Fruit getting comatose on Special Brew. We shaved off Egg's quiff while he was out for the count and drew on his face with a marker pen. Fruit's brother shaved off all Fruit's pubes as he slept and he never even woke up.

About 2 in the morning some of us wandered over the road, to the information tent. A giant inflatable room, like a bouncy castle but bigger. We climbed up it about 20 feet to the top, then slid back down again. What a ride. After ten minutes or so of playing, the coppers turned up.

'Get down!' they shouted,

'No!' we shouted back, 'Come and get us!'

This went on for a while, with us sitting on the top jeering, but they went away in the end, not very happy. We were though, we thought it was hilarious.

The flat got trashed and it looked like a bomb site in the morning, with about 15 people crashed out on the floor. Egg and Fruit were not very happy with their new 'hairstyles' and the landlord was not very happy with his flat either, but never mind, we were giving back the keys later on.

Damaged Goods

A couple of months later and my little sister got ill, whilst staying down in the south of France with a school friend's parents, at their holiday home.

Mum and Dad had booked to go on a holiday and I was the only other person who could go. Dad said he'd pay for the ferry, petrol and spending money if I went to get her and I jumped at the chance, who wouldn't? It was my first proper adventure.

I drove across France in my little Golf, stopping off for a great night with Francis in Brive, finally arriving down in Gers where the family lived, in a town called Condom, which made me chuckle.

It was scorching hot there but her friends parents were good fun and seemed to like the odd drink or two. One night me and the Dad went to visit one of his farmer friends nearby for a drink. We had some walnut liqueur from the farmer which was illegal and very strong and the father got so pissed that I had to drive his MG home for him, along the dusty back roads. I wasn't in much better shape than him and almost ended up in a ditch, which luckily he thought was hilarious.

He turned out to be the father of the crazy guy who used to have the little house painted in Rasta colours, that I'd known years ago. I was careful what I said, but he told me all sorts of tales about him and I thought it was a very small world.

On the way back to England, me and my sister only got lost the once, in a blizzard crossing the mountains. Just when I'd given up hope of finding the main road again, we came across a restaurant in a big old barn. The owner let us in, even though he was closed and cooked us a lovely meal and we stayed until the snow had stopped outside. After giving us directions and waving us off, we made it back across France in the rain that had replaced the snow of the mountains with no further ado, and got back to England safe and sound.

A few weeks later the alternator and battery gave out on my car and I thought it very lucky it hadn't happened in France.

My car, lost in France just before the blizzard hit.

Damaged Goods

Me and Fruit and co all went to the Milton Keynes Bowl to see David Bowie in concert.

Some of Fruit's friends were doing security that day and charged us a fiver each, to scramble through a hole they'd made in the fence. That gig was worth every penny. We sat on the grassy slope with our cans of Red Stripe looking on as David Bowie stood there astride the stage in his baggy, 80's suits and looked every part of the rock god that he was, belting out all his latest songs, what an entertainer. It was so cool to have somewhere like that on our doorstep.

Back at home, a few weeks later, Mum and Dad split up and Dad moved out. Mum wasn't coping too well, unsurprisingly, and was finding it hard with my 2 sisters being there. I offered to move back in and give her a hand and though I guess I wasn't best placed to help anyone, it seemed like the right thing to do. It was hard for all of us. The one thing we'd all grown up with, whether we liked it or not, was them two being together and now it was gone.

I have to say that it didn't really come as much of a surprise to me, as a few weeks before I'd stayed the night and awoken to them rowing loudly on the landing. I didn't really understand what it was all about, but I did know that my sisters were still asleep in bed and in my own special style, I'd lost my temper and knocked Dad down the stairs. I was sorry as soon as I'd done it and sure it didn't really help matters much.

It was a real bad time for everyone and I guess those times always are. I stayed for a few months, and did the big brother thing, trying to help Mum out, but after things had calmed down a bit, me and Mum started grating on each other, which she certainly didn't need and it was time to look for somewhere else to live again. Mum bought a house on the Costa del Sol in Spain to cheer herself up and it didn't look like I would be going to visit anytime soon.

Me and the Scouser went to see Gary Glitter play at Aylesbury. He'd got a MK 3 Cortina, red with a black vinyl roof, bucket seats and a skull gear knob. It was a cool car. He had a bag of his Novocaine, it was clean and made your whole head go numb, not anxious and sweaty like speed and we spent the entire journey talking. I needed some escape.

The support was the original Glitter Band and we sang along to 'Let's get together again' at the top of our voices. I think apart from that we spent the entire gig talking, just babbling really, but no one said anything to us. He did look very heavy, he was. What a fast night.

I bought a car from one of the bikers. It was a red shark nose '73 Chevy Camaro and my sister got my old Golf. Excellent.

Me and my Chevy Camaro, Linford Manor recording studios.

A few weeks later I moved in with the Scouser. His girlfriend lived there too, as well as his sister. She had black and blue spiky hair and wore a studded leather jacket, and fishnets. She was a Gothic Punk and I thought she was gorgeous. She thought that I was a flash twat though, I had a yank motor and I sold drugs, so I guess I couldn't really blame her, I was just her brother's friend.

Damaged Goods

I never felt flash though, living in a little room again, it felt like I was running on empty and I tried to fill the space up with anything I could. They played Fleetwood Mac's 'Tusk,' Frank Zappa, The Cult and Lloyd Cole's 'Rattlesnakes.' I played Elvis, Tom Waits, Hawkwind and Yello and The Rocky Horror Soundtrack.

He'd sold his Cortina and had bought a pale blue 3.0 Ghia Granada now, like The Sweeney, another cool car and he had a bike as well, a Honda 750 four, which at night he'd ride up the front steps and park in the front room, in front of the fireplace. It had a 4 into 1 exhaust and was really, really loud. Biker Goth.

That was some house, it seemed like we were speeding all the time, the record player was always on and it was a lot of fun and just what I thought I needed.

Their Mum and Dad were great too, they ran a big trucker's cafe by the MK Bowl where we used to go and eat. Their Dad drove a Mercedes and was the head chef as well as the owner and it did a roaring trade.

There always seemed to be lots of mysterious deliveries round the back, with all sorts of their Liverpool relatives and friends turning up, always talking quietly and smiling to each other.

Sometimes, when there was a big gig on at the Bowl, they would charge people to park out the front and enlisted us as extra help. We'd usually be speeding our heads off and found it hilarious to serve all the coppers and security, with our little pinprick eyes.

They used to pay us as well as feed us and they were really good times, we all got on great. The Scouser even went on holiday abroad with my sisters as a sort of chaperone.

One night in the pub I was tripping, off my head for a change, completely flying. I was sitting talking slowly to the Scouser's sister at a little table. Vision were singing 'Lucifer's Friend' over the sound system and it all seemed like a dream to me.

I was looking at my hands whilst I was talking. They were amazing to me and I just kept turning them over and over when suddenly she got up and walked off. What did I do? I was looking after her longingly but I couldn't get up.

My mate Malc came over and said I freaked her out, answering her questions before she had asked them.

'Can you read minds?' he asked. Fuckin' ell. I wasn't sure!

We got back to the house and were all sitting in the front room. She was looking at me, freaking me out a bit now. She was playing Paul and Paula's 'Hey Paula' on the record player.

'Look' I said, pointing to a big print on the wall and as I pointed it fell to the floor with a crash. Fuck's sake!

She ran upstairs to her room and slammed the door.

'How the fuck did you do that?' asked Malc.

I didn't know, this was getting weird. Malc said I was fuckin' crazy and I thought he might be right, but we all saw it.

There was some 5 minute religious thing on the tele before it closed at midnight where a priest came on and just stared out of the screen. We all looked, waiting for him to say something, but after five minutes he still hadn't said a word. We started looking at each other, what the fuck's going on?

After what seemed like hours he said 'Your eyes are doves,' stared knowingly out of the screen and it was over. The screen went blank. Wow. We were stunned into silence.

We sat and listened to some of Malc's records; Ella Fitzgerald singing 'I wonder Why,' Dean Martin singing 'Little Old Wine Drinker Me.' Excellent stuff.

We tried to work out what the priest had meant, but it was very difficult when you were tripping. It became a catchphrase for us, when we were pissed off in the week,

Damaged Goods

waiting for the weekend – 'Remember, your eyes are doves' usually did the trick with giggles all round.

Even adverts seemed to take on new meanings when you were tripping. There was one for fairy liquid. 'It's all greasy auntie. – Jenny! – She's right you know!' Everything on tele seemed hilarious, but we never seemed to watch it when we were straight though.

We often went for midnight walks, tripping out of our heads around the new city. It wasn't finished and there were loads of fields not yet built on in those days. Between the city centre and the house there were roads that just stopped beyond underpasses, like in local hero Eddie Stanton's 'Milton Keynes We Love you, Like fuck we do' single. How good was that song? Very. We lived those lyrics. 'How can people find their way, when the roads don't go nowhere?'

It was still dark out there, lots of the streetlights weren't connected and we walked for miles sometimes. Stopping to climb up the skeleton of an unfinished office block, staring out across the half lit cityscape, there were just floors and pillars, with no outside walls.

I found myself leaning off the edge, hanging onto one of the concrete reinforcing posts, singing the doors L.A Woman -'City at night, City at night' at the top of my voice. I thought it was funny until the post bent slowly down under my weight and I suddenly found myself staring out into nothing. I was hanging 60 feet off the ground, oh Fuck! Malc leaned out and grabbed me round the waist and we fell back in, laughing.

On those walks every step seemed like an adventure and fear never came into it. On the way home we went down into the roundabout on the dual carriageway, which had just been planted with trees. It was like a little forest and we sat in there for hours, watching the cars trailing by, giggling and feeling like the famous five, except I don't think they did Acid.

Sometimes when we got home we bumped into the milkman who we knew from the pub and lived opposite us.

He was only young and some nights he'd come over to ours and get stoned, then we'd all hop on his milk float and go delivering the milk with him, tripping. That was good fun, though I'm not sure if people got what they'd ordered.

The Scouser would go off to work early in the mornings and I never knew how he did it. He welded the frames for the new buildings, thirty feet up in a harness and it seemed like a city built on partying to me. He was hardcore, Mr. Non Stop. We weren't though, sometimes me and Malc would go and wait for the 7 – 11 to open and get cans of Red Stripe for breakfast, then hit the café for a fry up and lose the rest of the waking hours in dreamland.

The curtains were always shut in that house. I had a job in the week working for my Dad at his electronics company in M.K. There were people there I had known since I was little and it was a happy little family.

127

Damaged Goods

Dad had got his own house in MK now and I used to go and visit him sometimes. We'd chat for ages about this and that and before I left he'd always ask if I was ok and sometimes let me go and fill my Chevy up on his account at the petrol station, or give me 20 quid. I thought it should have been me asking if he was alright really.

Sitting in the canteen one lunch time, I mentioned The Rocky Horror Show was playing on stage in London and the rest of the apprentices were up for it. So, we organised a date that weekend and dressed up, with makeup, fishnets and Basques and drove down to London, parking near the theatre.

Walking down Wimbledon High St. getting wolf whistled at by blokes outside a pub, I cracked my bullwhip at them and laughed back. It was a great night, kind of seemed like old times. Stopping off at the motorway services on the way back at 2 in the morning got us some real funny looks though.

After a couple of years I left my job at my Dad's place to do landscaping with my old friend Mark. It seemed like a good idea at the time, with more flexibility, which was getting awful handy. To be honest, I never was gonna be a shining example of the boss's son as still, after 2 years in the drawing office, I hardly knew one end of a resistor from another.

Mark got some great contracts from the council, OAP lawns and endless grass verges along those dual carriage ways, it was tractor and mower heaven, village stuff. I still kept in touch with some of my old workmates though and still visited the factory some lunch times, if we were working nearby.

One night, some of them came to a party at the Scouser's house. It was packed - we even had the bouncers from the pub. There were people inside, outside and even sitting over the road on the pavement. Everyone was tripping and we gave it out for free.

Some of them had a good time, but some didn't and I found one of the apprentices lying outside in the gutter looking at a puddle, going on about being in a swimming pool. I don't think he'd done acid before. Oh dear, when worlds collide.

My brother rang me up. He'd come back to England for a holiday. His mate Brad was having a leaving do at his house in Enfield, and had told him to bring whoever he liked. So, me, Malc and Paul the photographer went off down the M1 to meet them at a pub in Islington.

By the time we got there they were ready to go. Follow us they said, jumping into their M.G. That was easy for them to say, they weren't tripping. So, there we were, speeding across London, trying to follow their car through endless road works. Bloody cones, the Chevy was a bit big for slalom and it felt like a big spaceship dodging stars. We were all giggling when we finally arrived. Tumbling out onto the verge, laughing. You want to take it easy on those things said my brother. Yeah I said, I know.

We went in and there was Brad. One wall of the front room was covered by stacked up beer. I'd never seen so many cans. They all seemed very quiet. Mind you they weren't tripping. We only did half as I didn't want to embarrass my brother.

We started to talk to people after a while and they all seemed really nice. There was one guy who had just got married. His wife was a real babe. Brad started to sing 'Blue Heaven,' after a bit of persuasion. Everyone joined in, us too.

Suddenly a piece of cake flew past his ear and splatted on the wall. That was it. Everyone started. We were sitting quietly in front of the beer mountain. There was food flying everywhere, people cheering.

So much for quiet. It seemed to go on for ages. I think it did. When it finally stopped there was food everywhere and everyone was laughing like drains. We were amazed.

Damaged Goods

People started to drift off and Brad dished out sleeping bags and disappeared upstairs.

We were all lying in a line, still quietly drinking beer. Next to me was Malc and on the other side were the newlyweds. They seemed to be getting awfully amorous so I turned away. Pass us a beer mate said the guy. I turned back around and his wife was sitting on top of him, shagging him like there was no tomorrow. She sure was fit.

I was speechless but he just laughed.

'Great ain't she' he said.

'Sure is' I said, 'I can see why you married her.'

He just laughed and turned back to business. We still didn't know what to do so we rolled over until we finally got to sleep. Blimey. Londoners.

Malc met this girl, what a little honey, and after a few months they got married, just like that. Me and Emma went to the wedding and it was a great day, church and everything. It was lovely but I couldn't really see us following suit anytime soon, shame.

Me, Emma the disco dolly, Funky Colin and Daz ended up at a very weird party afterwards, after taking a cab and discussing loudly how we were going to get out and run, though we paid in the end. The cab driver looked relieved and so was I.

Emma was getting people to sniff a jar of Marmite and they were so off their heads they thought it was drugs of some sort. Mind you, there was a lot of stuff going round there, it made me giggle.

Malc and his lady moved to North Wales and they bought a farm. We said we'd visit soon but the summer just seemed to disappear.

Finally we got around to it.... Half a gram of whizz, all in one line, each. Our poor noses, that stuff stung like a bastard. Just to set us up for the drive you understand. It was Christmas 1985 and we were off to the Llynn Peninsula in deepest Snowdonia, a different country, proper escape.

We had a bag full of trips, black bombers, more whizz, Red Lebanese and cans of Red Stripe, two trays full. There were five of us in the car and we were ready.

We took the A5 all the way up to Shrewsbury, with the stereo from the flat rigged up on the parcel shelf, Blasting out Yello's 'One second' and Hawkwind endlessly playing 'Space Ritual.' That was one fasssst Chevy ride though, it seemed like minutes with all of us talking a hundred miles an hour. We stopped at the Five Horseshoes in Shrewsbury for food and more beers. The next part of the journey was going to be through Snowdonia National Park, in the dark, drunk and drugged up.

Mmmm. Two hours in and the thought finally hit me, we're lost. Oh fuck. It was very dark there, not like the city. More by luck than judgement we found a village. Halle-fuckin-lujah.

Through the sleet I saw a copper stood by a roundabout in a rain smock. I stopped and rolled down the window.

'Excuse me...' I said, it was wet outside and he bent down and stuck his head in.

'Lost are you boys?'

We had two Spliffs going and all of us had cans of Stripe. After we told him where we were headed I looked at him and was it me or was he smiling? Fuck, what did I do that for? He gave us directions, reached across me and took Paul's spliff, saying

'Not thinking of moving here are you boys?'

Damaged Goods

'NO,' we said in unison, staring at his uniform. We couldn't move. Someone coughed and I held my breath.

'Good' he said, 'If you lay off this you might find it quicker boyo.'

He took my can from between my knees, took the spliff from my mouth and took a long drag from it, drained the can in one go and roared with laughter.

'Night night boys, drive careful now' he said, as he walked off back into the gloom.

We sat there in silence and started to giggle. We laughed, we roared, we got out of the car. We couldn't speak we were laughing so hard as we leaned on the car for five minutes. We got soaked but we didn't feel the cold.

Finally we got in and were off again. Just as we were exiting the village, I saw the copper walking up his driveway. I had one of those horns that played Colonel Bogie, like the Dukes of Hazzard, It suited the Chevy. I gave him a blast and he slapped his knees with laughter. We waved. Welcome to Wales.

We finally arrived at The Farm at 0400, after we'd got lost again. We all got out and stretched. Malc didn't answer the door, so I peered in through the front window and saw him, sprawled out on the floor, still holding a half empty bottle of Jack Daniels. Oh bollocks. His drinking seemed to have got worse since moving to the middle of nowhere and what was funny once just didn't seem it now. He was married, what the fuck was he playing at?

Finally we managed to wake him, after almost breaking the front door down and we gave him a big line of speed and he soon perked up.

Tom Waits was on his stereo singing- 'In The Neighbourhood.' We'd bought everything for Christmas dinner in the boot and as we bought it in, he perked up some more. His wife came home, she was a district nurse, she was a diamond and I don't know how she put up with him, but we missed them both.

They cooked the food at 100mph, speeding and we ate a wonderful Christmas Dinner. We had Champagne and cocaine, we had Red Stripe. We watched a 'Doors' video and then we all slept a whole day. Happy Christmas? You better believe it baby.

Boxing Day morning and the phone went. I answered and it was punky Suzy. Jesus! She got the number from my mum. She said 'Happy Christmas,' but I didn't know what to say to her anymore so I just said 'Goodbye.'

Where did I have to go to escape and why did I keep finding things and people to escape from?

We went outside for a walk, where it was sunny and cold, but at least it wasn't windy. We wrapped up and strolled along the coastal path to Hells Mouth.

We had Red Stripe and spliffs and had all taken some acid, for a change. Everything looked black and white, like someone had turned the colour down. We sat and watched the sea and the winter sun for an eternity, looking across towards Anglesey and the sea was as flat as a millpond. Finally, when it started to get dark, we floated back to the farm. Wow man.

Me at Hell's Mouth, North Wales.

Damaged Goods

We went to the nearest off licence five miles away and we bought trays of beer, Champagne and Vodka and cigarettes. We almost cleaned the place out and the boot of the car was almost full. The owner laughed, we laughed and she said that she would close early. Happy Christmas we said. Ho Ho Ho!

Back in England my brother was back from America again. I went and picked him up in the Chevy, but he wasn't very impressed, he had a new one in the states. I only had 'Second hand wings full of patches' like that Hoyt Axton song. Never mind.

Dire Straits were the biggest band on the planet at that moment and I'd got two tickets for their show at the NEC. and a coach ride there and back.

'Brothers in Arms,' The Cult's album 'Love' and Yello's '80 - 85 In One Go' were the albums we were playing all the time, nonstop.

What a show, I didn't hear a bad note all night, they sure could play guitar.

I was getting into a lot of old 60's music. It's like there was something in there, a message for me, waiting. I wondered if I was starting to lose it, I'd done a lot of acid and it was all starting to get a bit heavy. It didn't start out like that though, I just knew someone who could get acid. Lots of it. And speed, lots of it. Fuckin Kilos. It was my old friend Tony.

We had Supermen, we had Omms, we had Pink Panthers, we had White Lightning. We had whatever we wanted and it was like Christmas every week.

Tony knew people everywhere as he'd been travelling since punk had finished. He'd been to India, Amsterdam and Germany. I'd stayed though and I knew everyone here. Word spread fast as Milton Keynes was still a new city, sprung out of the fields like some Wild West frontier town and it was wide open. Tony was happy for me to be the man as it kept him a secret, making it easy for him to network further afield.

He was quietly spoken and polite and he didn't need to shout to make himself heard as people listened to him, Chairman Tone.

Damaged Goods

There were Gangs of builders from up north living on site for two months at a time building the new city and they liked to work fast. I sold speed to them like there was no tomorrow, fuckin pounds of it and it was never ending.

It ended for Jock the builder though, he was caught in a pub car park with a boot full of speed and got ten years. Turned out it was only 19 percent pure too, bastard. They didn't mind him going inside as he was only selling poor quality stuff and though it took the heat off us, Big Steve said if he hadn't been nicked he would have ended up under the new dual carriageway, which our builders worked on nights and I thought he was only half joking.

Two years of hard work by me and Tony, with Big Steve as our introduction. He was from here and he knew everyone that we didn't.

He was ten years older than us and we knew him from boxing club when we were younger. He had a vicious temper, Soulboy Steve, he'd been chucked out of the A.B.A. for fighting someone in the audience, before a match.

He was going up to Wigan Casino when we were still in shorts, in his Loon pants and cap sleeves with an Adidas holdall full of uppers to sell. He was the man.

He never got into punk and we were out of it now, we were all just in it together and music's music, and everyone liked soul anyway didn't they? I did. Trust was not a problem between us three.

We got our gear out of Liverpool, it came in from Amsterdam to Essex and I had no idea who with, but it always turned up and was always good stuff, with no problems.

Friday, after I'd made the drop, I drove back to the house and was lying on the floor in the front room, tripping, with Frank Zappa on the stereo.

I'd done two supermen and they were real strong. I was seeing colours and I seemed to have lost the power of speech. I couldn't remember how to form words, I couldn't remember who I was, but that was the point.

I felt like I'd failed at everything I'd ever done, but I was good at this, I was the fuckin' man. It was my choice. It'd probably kill me, but that was the point too. Way to go.

I was selling between one and two thousand trips a week every week. I sent some down to my friends Fruit and co, who had moved to Brighton, through the post, we never even thought that we might get caught and we never did, somehow.

I heard The Zap Club was really swinging down there at weekends and kept meaning to go down there for a night out but never seemed to find the time.

Steve's crew sold a thousand of them on into London every week too, they were old hands at this game. I usually sold a kilo of speed a month and sometimes I'd sell black bombers too. Not many, just a couple of hundred maybe, depended what was about.

I'd also get Dexedrine sometimes, I'd buy them in bags of a thousand from my village friend the chicken farmer. It wasn't all Townie shit. They fed them to the chickens to keep them awake and lay more eggs, poor fuckers. I must remember not to eat eggs. Chicken Dexy's, they were four for a pound, cheap as sweets, but I still made a profit on those too. It seemed to be spiralling out of my control a bit and felt like it was all getting a bit too heavy.

The son of the head of the MK Drug Squad hung around with us sometimes, which wasn't favourite as everyone knew his dad was a copper. He tried to be bad like us, but was a twat really and never quite managed it.

Damaged Goods

He tried too hard and was always stoned, even in the daytime. We were a bit worried to be honest. One Saturday morning he got very, very stoned at his dad's house, whilst his dad was away for the weekend and thought it would be funny to go for a ride in his dad's brand new Opel Senator squad car.

He went for a drive alright, he came to our place!

'What the fuck do you think you're doing bringing that thing here you stupid c**t?' shouted Big Steve.

We told him to fuck off and on his way home, he was so stoned that he put it in a ditch. Now he was very stoned and very scared, so he phoned us.

Steve laughed and said he thought it was great. He had an idea. He had relatives who ran a scrap yard. Ten minutes later and his mate arrived with his breakdown truck. It was starting to get dark and he had hip hop blaring out of the window, some group shouting 'Jive assed motherfuckers' over backing tracks. I thought it was scary and violent and it sure wasn't Nancy & Lee.

We winched the Senator on the back, whilst the copper's son was crying.

'What am I gonna do now?' he wailed, 'My dad'll kill me!'

'No' said Steve, 'He won't, I've got a better idea.'

He pulled out a Polaroid camera and took one instant photo of the copper's son, stood crying next to his old man's Senator. Oh Goody...

Half an hour later we pulled in to Steve's Uncle's scrap yard and there was his uncle and one of his friends waiting.

'Right' said Steve.

'Right' said his uncle.

'Hmmm,' said his friend.

His uncle gave out sledge hammers and they started beating every panel, every light and every window. They did not pause for breath and they had sneers on their faces.

Steve was screaming 'C***s' as he swung his hammer, the sweat already pouring off his forehead. It was fuckin' terrifying. Disney's 'King of the Swingers' was now blasting out of Steve's truck, oh for fuck's sake.

Finally they stopped and apart from the stereo, it seemed eerily silent. The car was trashed. If it could bleed it would; to death. Hold on said Steve, he wasn't finished yet. He got his cock out and walked around the car, pissing all over it.

Right he said as his uncle dropped the grab onto it and crunch it went, into the crusher. Steve and his friend spat at it as the jaws closed and it was gone.

They did not have smiles on their faces as they kicked the side of the crusher. They stood there staring at it and it was not a nice look.

Their relationship with the police was not a good one, as Steve's dad had been a robber in London and died in police custody when he was eight.

We dropped off the coppers son and it was only three hours later. He could now say that he knew nothing about his dad's car and we now had that Polaroid and some insurance that he'd never tell daddy what we were up to.

Damaged Goods

Queen were playing at Knebworth with Status Quo. Now that sounded like a good day out, so I asked everybody if they fancied it. Big Steve and the bikers from the village pub all said yes and we all decided to go. Oh goody.

I knew they were not maybe the trendiest thing to like, but good music went above all that and Queen were certainly that, entertainers extraordinaire. After all, we'd all grown up listening to them, even Quo and not everything had to be about fashion, good times were good times.

I drove up to the village pub in my new toy. I'd bought a beach buggy and it was great. There was a big row of bikes parked outside when I arrived, gleaming. The bikers were sitting on the Patio drinking Red Stripe and the windows were open, with Rainbow's 'Since You Been Gone' blasting out from the jukebox.

Me and my buggy, 1986

The sun was shining and it looked like being an excellent day out, so I got myself a pint and five minutes later, Big Steve and his gang turned up. He'd got a Triumph Stag which was very 70's cool and he had two of his mates sat up on the rear and one in the front. Oh bugger, I never thought about a problem between bikers and soulboys, they were all my friends.

I could see some hard stares as they all got out though, so I went to the bikers and explained that these were good friends of mine, who'd come for a good day out with us. Steve was stood behind me.

'No problem son' he said, 'Let's party.'

Smiles broke out as he passed a couple of joints and a bag of coke around. Rush's 'The Spirit of Radio' was blasting out of the windows now - good guitar.

The atmosphere had got better and they were all talking, sounding like they were setting up deals. Thank fuck for that, it would've been kind of a long day otherwise. Then finally we were off. The landlord came out to wave us off to the strains of Jefferson Starship's 'Jane.' Ten- ten, we'd got ourselves a convoy. Wahoo!

The cruise up there was great, I had got Sam Cooke's greatest hits on my stereo and he sure could sing. We all parked up and got in just as the Quo started, got some drinks and went and sat up on the hill, just back from the front.

After a couple of pints we headed down, just as Quo were doing 'Rockin' All Over the World.' It seemed like everyone was smiling and it was great. I don't remember what order they played what, but I do remember everyone singing and clapping along to 'Sweet Caroline .' A bunch of Soulboys? Blimey. Then it was time for Queen.

The band was playing and it was dark, when suddenly there was Freddie, stood atop a giant double staircase, wearing an Ermine gown and a crown. What a star that man was. He was punching the air along with the thousands in the

Damaged Goods

audience, he shouted something that I couldn't hear and that was it, they started.

Wow! I stood spellbound for the entire set. I can't explain it but that was just the best thing I had ever seen, and I'd seen a few. Absolutely incredible, what a showman! It was one of those things for me and I don't think I was alone. Everyone seemed to be thinking the same thing and to know all the words, like I did.

At the end we left before the real crowds and the bikers sped off back to the village ASAP, for some after hours drinking.

I cruised home slowly in the buggy, the wind blowing in my hair, mixing with the Grace Jones cassette on my stereo.

I came off the main road and turned up towards the village and there was smoke everywhere. I could see flames here and there, all along both sides of the road. Blimey, what's going on?

They were burning stubble I realised. I'd forgotten about that, had I been away that long? Felt like a lifetime ago that I was a village boy. It looked medieval or something and I suppose it must have looked much the same then. Bloody great I thought, but I was glad I wasn't tripping for once.

I pulled off the road through an open gate and parked on the edge of a field and sat there looking at it, smoking a fag. Through gaps in the smoke I could see how far it went on, bloody miles it looked like. I was sitting there with the stereo off, humming Elvis songs, when out of the smoke a figure loomed. It was one of the farmers from the village. 'Oh it's you,' he said. He had two rabbits dangling over his shoulder and a 12 Bore in his hand.

'Look' he said, 'Smoked rabbit!'

He collapsed in fits of laughter, so did I, silly fucker. He asked me what I was up to and I said that I just wanted to look for a bit if that was alright.

142

'OK' he said, 'But don't be doing any rabbit impersonations' and told me I was a nutter.

'I know' I said, 'I know, fuckin' tell me about it!'

He walked off into the smoke laughing. I just wanted to remember this day and get it fixed in my mind. A whole adventure with no drugs, I didn't do them in the daytime. I wasn't a junkie. I think I just wanted to remind myself of that, so I sat there smoking and looking out across the fields for a couple of hours, thinking. Who the fuck am I? I'm not a city boy but not really a villager anymore either, like a square peg in a round hole.

I felt I was drifting through life, lost, without a purpose. I was thinking about Don Juan saying 'Choose a path with heart' but it was a job to see one through all the smoke. I've got that phrase tattooed on my chest, in French - 'Choisir le chemin avec coeur.'

Much later I cruised back up to the village to stay at Mum and Dad's for the night. It wasn't easy driving quietly in a beach buggy with an unsilenced VW engine, but I did my best. Bed. I fell asleep listening to Meat Loaf's 'Bat Out of Hell' L.P.

Damaged Goods

A week or two later and I was driving to Tony's in the buggy, with a grand in my pocket and 500 trips. I came up to one of the new roundabouts that wasn't planted yet and just had a curb round it. I looked in my rear view mirror and saw something zooming up behind me. Ha ha, did he want a race? Watch this! I dropped a gear and floored it and jumped straight over the roundabout.

Now there was a flashing blue light in my mirror. Oh fuck. I pulled over, not much choice really, this wasn't the Dukes of Hazzard. A copper walked up and I got out. He was laughing. It was fuckin' Geoff, I couldn't believe it!

He was shaking his head.

'What the fuckin' ell was that?' he asked.

I told him I was sorry and I didn't see it was a cop car.

'I guessed that,' he said, 'Is it yours and is it all legal?'

'Yes' I said.

'Tell me you're not pissed this time either,' he said.

No, luckily I wasn't.

'Well I'm gonna have to do you for something' he said, 'My colleague wasn't very impressed with your stunt driving.'

He walked around it and got his pad out and wrote me a speeding ticket and something to present my documents at the station.

Then he told me to fuck off and not do it again, but he was still laughing. He also told me to try and drive round roundabouts. I hopped in and he stuck 2 fingers up at me as I roared off.

Fuckin' ell, that was close, as I adjusted the packet in my pocket. I always thought I had a guardian angel, but never thought it would be dressed up as a copper.....

What you get for jumping straight over a roundabout, if you happen to know the copper!

One week later. I was with Tony again, driving to the City Centre in the Chevy, carefully. Something cruised past us, what the fuck is that? I could not believe my eyes. It was a giant brontosaurus skeleton doing sixty miles an hour up the dual carriageway.

It passed and Tony said it was 'The Mutoid Waste Company.' They made giant sculptures from rubbish he said and they've come to town. So we followed them to the centre. They parked outside the YMCA, got out and walked over.

Damaged Goods

They said they were staying for a week. We asked them if they fancied having a party and said we'd get the acid and the sounds.

'You're on' they said. 'Fancy a ride?'

It was a long lorry chassis and running gear, with this Skeleton thing sculpted on top. It looked like nothing I'd ever seen. We cruised around the city centre for a while and got lots of looks, with some people looking scared, like they were afraid it might bite.

Saturday came and we'd spent the whole week calling people from all over. The Mutoids had camped down by Caldecotte lake, there were no estates finished down there yet, just building sites. They'd been scouring them for rubbish and they'd made all these giant sculptures from all the old pipes and stuff they had found.

Weird was not the word. The encampment looked like something from a Sci-Fi nightmare and that was in the daytime, straight, I couldn't wait to see it tripping.

We set up the sound system and fuck me it was loud. Still there wasn't anyone to annoy round there. They were looking at my car and asked if I fancied a row of red shark fins, front to back across the bonnet roof and boot. They weren't kidding. 'I'll see' I said.

All of a sudden it was evening and people started turning up, hundreds of them. Big Steve and the Trendies from the nightclubs, my Scouse friends with all the local Goths, Hannah and Matt with Rita and Sharon, even my little sister and her friends. Blimey there's Steve Spon from UKDecay with the Luton lot and some of the old Leighton lot. Seemed like everyone was there, Uncle Tom bleedin' Cobley and all.

The music was really going some, with Toots and the Maytals. Ska Music blasting out loud from the sound system, which was in a big marquee, don't know where that came from.

Down by the speakers there was someone dancing with his arms stretched out, like he was flying and I guess he was.

Good Acid he said. He was right, it was good acid and there were hundreds of us tripping.

That place looked surreal in the dark, there were so many people there and the night just seemed to go crazy. Some Gypsies started fighting with tent poles from the marquee for some reason. We'd invited them as they bought loads of acid from us. Luckily no one really got hurt as they were all too out of their heads, but it wasn't a good vibe for a while.

We went for a burn around the lake on the skull bus, with about 20 of us hanging off the sides like a troop carrier, Me, Douggie & Neeta, Mattie and Paul the photographer, Tony & Spon, don't know who else. The driver was tripping off his head too, driving it. How can you do four wheel drifts on the grass in a lorry?

Me in the Mutoid Waste Company's Skull Bus.

Damaged Goods

I got convinced that he was going into the lake as he careered towards the edge, as did Mattie and Paul and we jumped off doing about 30 miles an hour, rolled along for a bit then got up. No-one was hurt and we were all laughing. We looked up and watched the bus. It didn't go in the lake after all but instead zoomed across the top of the weir to the other side, which was just wide enough. Then, with headlights swooping through the dark, they all disappeared off round the other side of the lake. Oh bollocks I thought, we should have stayed on after all, but never mind, that jump sure was exciting.

It started to piss down with rain. Me and Douggie had military trench coats on and we decided to leave the Chevy and walk back to Mattie's, it was only four miles and we fancied an adventure and I could always pick the car up the next day, probably safer.

The city looked good slicked in rain and the neon kinda suited it. We stopped by a storm drain watching the water swirl around under a streetlight. As I looked, I could see all the letters of the alphabet swirling around in it, but of course I could, I was tripping. I told Douggie and Neeta and they said they could see them too! This stuff was great.

We watched for about half an hour before we walked off, finally getting back to Mattie's about 3 am, soaked but happy. We'd hardly drunk a drop all night and fell asleep in the dark on the sofa, all cuddled up together, listening to JJ Cale's 'After Midnight.'

The acid was starting to bring up memories I had forgotten and sometimes they ran through my mind like a film. I saw it all when I was awake and I saw it all on the back of my eyelids when I slept. My whole life seemed to be being lived all at once. I remembered everything from the age of two onwards and I wished I didn't, as it wasn't all good, not at all. I sometimes wondered if I was dreaming. It was becoming a fuckin' nightmare.

Malc was back for the week from Wales, staying on the sofa. Wales was going tits up he said and I wasn't really surprised, but Jesus! How could all this be better? What was wrong with him? I got the feeling I wasn't even getting half the story. He stole cars, he stole everything.

He was leaning over me, trying to get me up. I was tripping again, 2 Supermen. I couldn't speak; I couldn't understand what he was saying to me. It was like every word stretched. I couldn't remember how to move my legs and I was seeing colours.

The taxi was waiting to take us to the pub. Malc lifted me in a fireman's lift and carried me out to the taxi. It was half past seven at night and the taxi driver laughed, saying I should be like that at the end of the night, not the start. Malc told him to fuck off and said I'd be fine, just drive. He was right and as we walked in I came round, sort of. I could speak and walk slowwwwly. I was floating and people seemed pleased to see me. Of course they were, I was the man. The Cult were playing 'Phoenix' over the sound system - 'Well dig this.'- and I sure was baby.

On Friday nights it wasn't business, not really. I could afford to give away 20 trips for every 100 that I sold and still make a profit.

I went to the bar and someone pushed in front of me and knocked me out of the way, it was a big biker.

Steve appeared. He wasn't long back from six months in prison and he looked like it, with scars and bleached hair. He'd got a new suit and looked 80's Ssssharp, with big shoulder pads and 'Kouros' aftershave. He looked like a Mastiff with a diamond collar as he pulled his jacket off and threw it on the floor. He'd got half a pool cue in his hand and it seemed to fan out from his arm as he swung it, trailing. Course it did, I was tripping.

The biker got a broken nose and he said sorry to me. He said he was wrong and I was first at the bar. I felt sorry for him, but he was right and I thought he was very lucky he

Damaged Goods

didn't get his blood on Steve's clothes, as Steve put his jacket back on.

It was like I was untouchable. I never asked for this. I used to be able to look after myself and still could if I had to. It was just that....it was just that... I seemed to be out of my head all the time lately.

I ordered ten bottles of Grolsch from the bar, as I didn't want to come back and have to try and speak to the barmaid again later and went and sat down.

A few hours later as I went to leave, Steve gave me the keys to an XJS that was parked outside. It was brand fuckin' new and didn't even have a number plate on it. I said I couldn't drive it, I said I was fucked. He laughed and said it didn't matter, but don't leave prints. There was even a pair of driving gloves on the dash. He said if you're caught, just leave it and run, but if you crash it, just set fire to it and then run. He said it didn't matter, it was going to be trashed tomorrow anyway. I had no idea what he was on about, but I took the keys and said thanks.

I was sitting at a table with everyone, Mattie, Hann, Douggie, Neeta, Malc and Big Steve. With bottles and pint pots everywhere. It was like our own private club.

There were people asking for trips and I had fifty in my pocket but I couldn't get them out. I couldn't remember how. Malc did it for me, he even puts the money in my pocket when they were all sold, he didn't steal from me. Someone said they wanted 500, sure, see Steve tomorrow I said, we'll do it no problem.

The DJ put on The Art of Noise and Duane Eddy – 'Peter Gunn.' He said it was for me. I waved and he smiled back. He was tripping too, there were at least 20 people tripping in here that I knew of. That twangy guitar just seemed to bend around the room. Then he put on an American rap band, 'Hawk' singing 'The Alarm' – 'Get up Motherfucker, Get out of your bed.' Rap and heavy guitar, years before Aerosmith and Run DMC.

It was great. I was still sitting at the table with the crew, staring at my beer. I was staring for 10 minutes, with everyone talking around me because I couldn't move my arms, couldn't remember how. Malc noticed and he lifted the bottle up, put my fingers around it and laughed. I laughed too. I was fine then. Aha were singing 'The Sun Always Shines' and I thought 'Fuckin' tell me about it!'

A night in The Pilgrim's Bottle, MK.

The big ceiling fans felt like a gale, they felt warm, I felt like I couldn't breathe. The rush was wearing off, after 3 hours, wow man – what a hit!

We left the pub at midnight with no thought of the state we were in. This was normal for us, well no it wasn't really, we didn't do normal. We were immortal, we were untouchable, we knew everyone and everyone knew us.

Damaged Goods

The Jag was Gold, it was gleaming and it was ours for the night. It felt like Cinder-fuckin-ella, was it going to turn into a pumpkin? No, probably a cube of scrap metal, but it could turn into a ball of flame if I wasn't careful. Mmm, the thought registered, better be careful then.

Six up, doing 110 mph in the fog and I couldn't see more than 20 feet in front of me. Yello were blasting out of the sound system with 'St. Senor the Hairy Grill' and it's manic guitar, and that was heavy. It was like driving underwater. This was careful; no it wasn't, we didn't do careful.

As we slowed for the roundabout, a Mini Van roared past us as if we were standing still. I knew that car, it was my mechanic friend from the next village and he'd fitted a Rover V8 into that Mini, it went like stink. They couldn't believe it and I wasn't going to spoil it by telling them. He'd always been gifted with cars.

Back onto the new Dual carriageway and a pair of red fog lights loomed up in front of me out of the fog, just before our junction and I cut across them from the fast lane up the exit ramp, thinking it was my mate in his Mini, but, as we flashed past I looked over at the driver and he looked at me. It was a moment. It was a police Sierra. Oh fuck, but too late now, we were gone up the ramp and he was off into the mist.

I was still doing sixty as we approached the roundabout at the top and I forgot it was an auto. I stuck it into reverse by mistake while we were still doing 30 and Bang! The car jumped in the air. I know I was tripping but I swear it did! - two feet off the ground! It landed on the curb of the roundabout rocking, still running somehow and I was sitting there wondering if we should call Jaguar to tell them how strong their cars were. I think my thought processes weren't quite right anymore.

Still, there we were and we were all ok. We got out and were standing on the roundabout thinking of torching it, when a car pulled up. Luckily it wasn't the Police, it was Steve. He was laughing at the car. He had a friend with him who had a long scar down his face and he was laughing too.

They had Golden Earring playing 'Radar Love' in their car and it drifted across the roundabout as we all pushed it off the curb.

We got back in and it clonked a bit when I put it in drive, but the fuckin' thing still drove!

'It won't tomorrow morning,' Steve said, 'We're taking it to the crusher.'

Him and his friend. Lots of things ended up in that scrap yard so I'd heard.

'Don't fall asleep in it!' they said and I really didn't think they were joking.

Finally we got home and sat smoking opium laced black before crashing out. It was the only time I smoked that stuff, I didn't like it but it always made me sleepy. I put 'Nancy and Lee' on the stereo singing 'Summer Wine' and I slept like the dead.

Weeks later I moved out of the Scouser's house when I saw something I didn't like and I moved in with Hannah and Matty.

Friday, I was down the pub, tripping as usual. I'd got faded 501's tucked into my embroidered cowboy boots, black polo neck, faded Denim jacket, studded Punk belt and bleached hair.

The Scouse girl came up to me and asked me why I didn't move back in and told me she missed me. My head was flying. What? Then she said she loved me and I didn't know what to say. I was having trouble thinking and I couldn't believe what I was hearing. I thought she didn't like me. She told me I was a fookin' twat and then she kissed me. Wow. It seemed to go on forever, that was some kiss and I felt it in my boots. In front of everyone. How long had I wanted to do that?

I was stood there speechless and the D.J. put on Charlie Whitehead singing 'I Finally Found Myself Something to Sing About,' one of Steve's Northern Soul 45's. Oh very

Damaged Goods

funny! I stuck two fingers up at Steve and he laughed and for the first time I wished I wasn't tripping. Oh fuck.

The DJ was playing more Northern Soul – George Tindley singing 'Pity the Poor Man' and there was Steve and two of his mates. Fuck could they dance. They were spinning, doing back flips and jumping scissor kicks on the beat. Steve always said that Disco was watered down Soul and I could see what he meant. That was impressive.

Everyone was looking on and I don't know what they were seeing but I was tripping and Steve's feet were a blur. They were all off to London tomorrow, where the 6T's Northern Soul Club were having an all-nighter on a boat, with a dance floor and everything. Blimey.

The next day when I woke up I wasn't sure if it had really happened. But the next week she was there again and again she kissed me. I wished I'd known for sure that she'd be there, If I could think straight I'd do something. But of course, I was tripping again.

I'd lived there for a year and had been crazy about her, but it was too late. My head was fucked now, I couldn't help it. I was tripping all the time. It blocked things out, like me, like pain. So I did nothing about it and I think she took that badly. She was pissed off with me and I was pissed off with myself.

It was like I'd started something I couldn't control anymore, it wasn't addiction but... If I stopped I'd have nothing and I'd have to face myself, just when I'd found a new way to avoid it.

It was my childhood coming back to haunt me and I knew that now, I couldn't kid myself when I was tripping.

How would I live, how could I live with her, how would we afford it? I couldn't think beyond that, but maybe I should have. Oh fuck, what was I doing? I knew at the time I'd always regret it and I was right, I have. I knew what was waiting for me at the end of it all too now... Me.

The following week Hannah and Mattie had organised a surprise for her boyfriend Pat.

'Wanna come?' they asked.

I like surprises, so the following week we all set off in Hannah's Cortina estate, but just down the road it ran out of petrol. We got out to push it to the petrol station and Pat turned to me and said this was fun.

'You ought to try it tripping' I said.

'You're not are you?' he asked, laughing.

We got it filled up but it still wouldn't start, so Hannah went up to some guy at the till and asked if he'd got some jump leads. He did have and so would I, Hannah sure looked nice in her denim miniskirt and big 80's hair. Mmmm.

We were off and the drive seemed to go on forever. The giggle mobile. Finally, we were there and Pat had his eyes closed as we went into the theatre, me too. We sat down in the dark and suddenly the lights came on and The Drifters walked on stage, all white tuxedos and white smiles.

The Drifters! Wow! I sat mesmerised as they sang 'Under the Board Walk' 'Saturday Night At the Movies' and all their other hits. I'd been listening to them since I was little and it was like a dream to actually see them.

They never stopped smiling for the whole gig and neither did I. They were so cool and I don't know who enjoyed it more in the end, me or Pat, but that was some trip.

Damaged Goods

Friday and me, Mattie and Paul the photographer went to Douggie & Neeta's for the night.

Tripping as soon as we got there, we went for a walk in the woods. The sand on the paths was glowing and we were all giggling, doing silly walks. We felt warm and safe. We ended up in a field with piles of hay bales everywhere, as it was harvest time. We jumped on them, falling over and it seemed like a fairground ride. The starlight seemed really bright and we played for ages, ending up sitting under some trees in the middle of the field. We lay on our backs looking at the stars and I couldn't stop laughing, the world just all seemed so funny.

Me and Douggie on the way home from the woods.

Later on, when we were walking along the country lane back into the village, we saw an old Victorian streetlight. Douggie put his hand up to point at it and something flew around his outstretched arm. It was a bat, blimey!

'Look' he said, 'They're playing with us.'

We all stuck up our hands and more bats came and circled round and round. Wow, we thought, ain't nature great? We watched spellbound as they flitted and swooped endlessly and Douggie was right, they were playing with us.

The bats left after about half an hour, though it seemed longer and we walked back to Douggie's house. It looked really weird and tall when we got there and we all stopped and stared up at the roof, it didn't look that tall in the daytime.

'Not 'cause we're tripping then,' said Douggie, laughing.

'Oh Yeah, I forgot!'

We went in and put on a Marc Bolan video of him singing a duet of 'Life's a Gas' with Cilla Black. It was beautiful, she was staring into his eyes, 'ahhh' we all said and fell asleep as it was getting light outside, with the birds singing to us and they sounded beautiful too.

The following week it was my birthday. I had a party in the newly opened pub in MK, The Barn. My family and friends all turned up and someone had organised a roly poly strip-o-gram for me. She was a big lady, who proceeded to strip both her and me down to our undies, before bending me over a chair and whipping me. What could you do?

It was like being in a bad 501 advertisement, but good fun and it made a change to be somewhere different.

Later on, after my family had left, we all took a trip, for a change, and went and sat outside.

Paul the Photographer was looking up and down at the streets and buildings and saying wow a lot. I asked him if he was ok and he said he was great and that he could see all the perspectives of the city, like in an architect's drawing, in a way he'd never seen before.

He wandered off snapping away with his camera and he's been travelling and photographing stuff ever since really, with some fantastic photo books published on many of the world's major cities.

Damaged Goods

It was Saturday lunch time and me, Tony and the chicken farmer were in the pub, with The Talking Heads singing 'Psycho Killer' on the jukebox. We all agreed that selling the Chicken Dexy's was good, but there was something else we could do which would make a lot more money, now that we had some to put in.

The farmer had a burger van that did quite well, but it wasn't big enough to cook for big events and Tony said he wanted one for Glastonbury. We had the money and the farmer had a festival licence, so the farmer thought about it for a few minutes and said yes, why not? He said he'd work it with us if we got it built. We wanted to sell all sorts from it, the deal was done and Summer was on the way. Yum Yum Yum!

2 months later and the trailer was ready, it sure looked fine and it should have done too. Steve knew a catering equipment manufacturer that he went to school with and he had built us the best looking food trailer you ever saw, with more turned aluminium than a vintage Bentley!

It was the dogs bollocks. The sign had 'Yummy Zoomers' painted over the serving hatches, which was an in joke you'd understand, if you were an acid casualty, like us.

We had a bag full of novocaine and bombers and were playing Motorhead's 'No Sleep Til Hammersmith' in the trailer.

We wouldn't be getting much sleep that weekend either, we were selling burgers, hotdogs and chips, but we were also selling Novocaine and Trips too. No one else on the site was selling Novocaine or Trips like ours, Tony had made sure of that with his friends from Amsterdam. They were in charge for now and Tony said he had bought a house there through them, on the canal.

The money poured in and the sweat poured off. I think Simply Red were on the main stage but it was hard to make it out and anyway we didn't stop for the music, we weren't there for fun. We did manage to have some though -

anything that dropped on the floor was put on a special shelf, after we'd trod and spat on it and if any customers gave us any hassle we served it to them, as an extra free portion.

'Here you go mate, Have a double on us!' to cheer them up. Then they always said that they were sorry they'd been stroppy. They would be by the next day, when they'd be queuing for those lovely toilets with the shits. All served up with a smile, Ha Ha Fuckers!

Later on, as it calmed down, Aswad were playing and me and Emma the disco dolly went for a shower. She was so beautiful, she looked like Nancy Sinatra but prettier, with 60's hair and big blue eyes. Aqua Marina, Brigitte Bardot, Blondie, Mmmm.

I guess she was what you might call a Suicide blonde, but hers was a long story and not mine to tell. I'd known her since we were little at the old village disco's and she came to Glastonbury with me, wearing a cocktail dress and stilettos. Very 80's.

How did she end up with a drug dealing ex punk rocker? I couldn't really remember but it was at one of my parties and I was so happy, I had always fancied her. The disco dolly and the punk, I think my life was turning into a fairy tale and maybe it was a village thing I thought.

We queued up nervously, as we'd never been in a communal showers before, full of bloody hippies. I'd never really worried about the size of my cock before, as it wasn't exactly something that filled my thoughts, but if I was going to, now was the time.

There we all were, stripping off and into the showers before I got the chance to worry too much. Men and women all naked, only feet from each other and with the beautiful Emma next to me, I glanced over at the guy on the other side, as you do.

He was looking over at Emma and he was all tattoos and biceps. I looked down, as you do, and saw that he'd only got a tiny little cock! I just about stopped myself from

Damaged Goods

laughing and looked the other way, where a big Rasta was scrubbing away, he must have seen me checking and was chuckling, giving me the thumbs up.

He turned back to his shower head and I scrubbed away with carefree abandon after that. Whatever, it's better than the communal toilets -all that dodgy food......!

We managed one walk around the site all weekend as we were so busy it was almost disgusting. The food wasn't though, the meat was from the village and we sold good quality stuff, like our drugs.

The Psychedelic Furs were singing 'India' on our built in sound system and it was going so well, it was decided that we'd have an ice cream van too next year- 'Uncle Yummer's Ices.' I wasn't sure if it was still funny. It sounded like the child catcher from Chitty Bang Bang and seemed a bit sinister to me, selling drugs from an ice cream van - Childhood's End. We didn't do kidnap and cages though, I'm glad to say.

Fuck's sake! We made over 50,000 quid in cash that weekend. Steve was burying himself in it in his front room and we were all laughing like we couldn't believe it, which we couldn't.

That was an awful lot of money back then, you could buy a house with it and Steve did, well, a flat anyway. Tony had opened a bank account in Luxembourg for the rest of us and we fed that fucker.

So, one month later round at Steve's we were listening to James Brown 'Get On The Good Foot,' whilst Steve was talking to someone on the phone. He wanted to take the trailer to Silverstone, to sell Coke to the rich people. He wants more. Bloody Hell, him and his cars, mind you I was as bad. This wasn't a game and he wasn't scared of Prison,

'It comes with the job' he said, so fuck' em, let's do it.

He wanted to buy a house in Spain and some hotels. His friends from London were already out there doing well.

'It's where the money is' he said 'And the sun. It's like Miami Vice except the coppers are all bent and you can buy whatever you want down there.'

Steve wanted a Corvette and a pool, like me, but I always thought I'd be the good guy and I'd never even thought about Coke really. There hadn't been a master plan that I knew of but I guess that shit happens.

Me and Emma went down to her dad's place for the weekend to get away. He lived in a village near Torquay and was entering his powerboat in the Cowes - Torquay race. He had some house, a 4 car garage with a Ferrari 308, a Jensen SP111 and an E type Jag in it. There was even a fuckin' helicopter on the lawn - Wow!

We had a swim in his pool before eating supper out on the terrace. He looked like Frankie Vaughan. Emma said he built houses, amongst other things, he seemed to be doing very well.

We went into town for Lunch the next day as he owned the local pub too and I noticed that the people there seemed to have a lot of respect for this man, it almost seemed like fear if you know what I mean, but I didn't ask questions. We got on like a house on fire though and he was great.

We spent the rest of the day out on his Yacht, watching him in the race. His powerboat made it to Cowes in very good time, but broke down halfway back. He said it didn't matter to him though, it was just fun to be there as he'd grown up dreaming of being rich. I liked this man. I think he liked me too.

The next day he took us for a ride in the powerboat as it had only been a fuelling problem he said. Fuck's sake, that thing was fast.

'Keep your knees bent' he said, 'Otherwise you might break your neck,' and he wasn't kidding!

Damaged Goods

I couldn't see the speedo and was hanging on for dear life as it took off over a wave. When it landed it felt like we'd hit a rock and then all of a sudden he was wheelying it. It was a fuckin boat! Jesus, what a buzz! 'Sure is!' he said, laughing.

He asked me to move down there with Emma and said he'd set me up with a house and a job as it'd be great to have his little girl down there. Emma said no though as she still lived with her mother in our village, shame. I was starting to think I'd had enough of my lifestyle and was starting to think that I might want a normal one. I wondered if there was enough of me left to sort out. Hmmm...

I was starting to hear rumours about Emma but I chose to ignore them, she wouldn't would she? I remembered her from when we were little, but we never went to the same school. When I danced with her at the village disco I was 14 and she was 11 and everyone had laughed.

I had loved her from afar but I guess maybe I didn't really know her after all. I might have noticed if I'd been straight, as Big Steve had told me she was messing about ages ago, but. I didn't want to hear it, I wanted it to be right. Right? What was I thinking? I was drugged up most of the time and she drank me under the table every night, all five beautiful feet of her. I didn't know where she put it.

She was with me most nights, like peas in a pod, except for her girl's nights out when she stayed at her girlfriend's house. Didn't she? No she didn't. Finally I found out. Oh Fuck. Gone wrong again. I guess I couldn't blame her though if I was honest, but it hurt to be honest and that's why I tried to avoid it.

Two wrongs don't make a right and I was definitely going wrong, so was Emma and I wasn't helping her - I don't think anyone could, though plenty tried it seemed.

I thought my Fairy Tale was becoming one of the Brothers Grimm and I probably deserved it. I was starting to wonder if there were any happy endings, probably not for a drug dealer eh?

Maybe I should start to write my own, but that would have meant stopping wouldn't it, then what would I have? This was all I had and I knew it was all wrong, but it was a world that we'd made for ourselves and I loved those guys. I didn't want to be alone again.

There's a Gene Vincent song 'Hurtin For You Baby' and the words just about summed it all up for me at that moment, check out the second verse.

Damaged Goods

One week later we were round at Tony's, with the Cramps 'Faster Pussycat' playing on his stereo, when the farmer rang up with a problem. The trailer had gone, stolen!

Uh oh! You would have seen a switch go in Steve's head if you'd been there, it was like that - F words as his fist went through the glass of the kitchen door, there were blood and glass shards everywhere.

'Right!' he screamed,

'I'm gonna find that fucker!'

I believed him. Tony was sitting with his hard stare on, Chairman Tone, it was indeed a hard stare - he didn't like it when people messed up his arrangements. I didn't know which one was more scary! Oh goody, this should be fun.....

Actually it wasn't. Steve found out where it was. It turned out that the gypsies that we sold acid to had pinched it, so...

I remember what happened next in little flashes.

There were six of us, black bombers and no beer, nice clear heads. The land rover smelled of diesel with things clunking in the back as we went over bumps along a track. We had pickaxe handles and swords, fuck me, this wasn't playing.

It was dark as we arrived at their encampment and there sat our trailer. Steve poured a jerry can of petrol over it, setting fire to our own trailer in front of the people who nicked it.

'Fuck it' said Steve, 'It's insured. 'You wanted it, you can fuckin' have it' he shouted at them.

That was the first time I saw Steve pull a gun and he shot one of them in the legs, just like that. One of them started to pull out a sawn off next to me, looking at Tony with murder in his eyes. I did him with a pickaxe handle before he could point it and just about took his head off.

There were a lot of people screaming and we set fire to their barn. I didn't say a single word, quiet one me, but what do you say anyway? Until we got back to Steve's, then I said I didn't think it was a good idea to start a war with Gypsies. He said he didn't think it was a good idea for them to start one with us. OK, about right I supposed, but whatever, fun is not a word I would have used.

Damaged Goods

OK I needed a rest from all the madness of the new city, it was getting to me, I was just a village boy at heart. I was walking in the woods with Douggie when a thought came to me. The pathways were sand like a beach and the trees were pines. Mmmm. You could have a pretend beach party down there. Wouldn't that be funny!

I spoke to Douggie and he was into it, so we planned it for the weekend, just me and him and his wife, Neeta. We went down there Saturday morning and collected logs for a fire and I spent all week making cassettes of music that we loved, T. Rex, The Velvet Underground, The Doors and Nancy Sinatra & Lee Hazelwood.

Me and Mattie got to Douggie's house about 8 o'clock in the evening. Mattie had brought a load of Red Stripe, Douggie & Neeta had rolls and potatoes in tin foil and hand painted jam jars with candles in, to hang from the trees. I brought Acid, Supermen and we took a tab each and then set off to the woods.

We got the fire lit before the trip started working, by which time it was getting dark. The fire was big and we sat around it, looking at forever in the flames. The Velvet Underground were singing 'Candy Says,' they were singing 'Stephanie says,' they were singing 'Lisa says,' one after the other. The music was soooo mellow, it sounded too slow, it sounded great, course it did, it was my tape.

Fuck that stuff was strrrrrong. My stomach was churning and I could see and hear everything all at the same time. Time and place disappeared. So did I. Douggie was crying and Neeta told him she loved him. I told him I loved him. Douggie said it was too strong and he was right, it was.

Blimey, I'd done 3 at a time before that hadn't felt as strong as they did that night. I told him it would be alright and took him to the steep grass bank next to us.

'Look at the stars Douggie' I said, it was all I could think of.

He lay down and looked up and was suddenly silent for what seemed like forever. He was smiling. 'See?' I said. 'Yeah' he said. We all lay down there for a while looking up at the stars.

The Doors were playing. 'Crystal Ship' and the music seemed to swirl up into the night sky with the flames and sparks from the fire. It was the night of the shooting stars and it was like a firework show.

There seemed to be hundreds of meteors up there and little clouds scudding across the stars. They looked pink, they looked orange and they made patterns. The Crescent moon was hanging contentedly, looking like a stage prop, it was a stage prop, we could see the wire! It was an American fifties moon from a stage show, with a big smiling face.

Course it was, we were tripping. 'Strange Days' drifted up into the night and suddenly there was a moment. We were all smiling, we could see the meaning of life, all of it, all at once. We all had the same thought and were all crying all of a sudden, we were so happy.

A couple of hours later, that seemed like years, it was still dark and the trip wasn't so intense. The candles were glowing in their jars, the colours were beautiful and it looked like a fairies party in the woods.

I could see sparks in the other's eyes as we danced around the fire to T.Rex singing 'Get It On.' I was flailing my arms slowly like a windmill and could see ten arms fanned out, trailing like the special effects on old Top of the Pops, wow! We all had a go. We loved Marc Bolan and were suddenly sad that he'd gone. The music seemed to be coming from all around us as Marc sang 'Life's a Gas.' It was.

Neeta climbed a little silver birch tree, it was only 4ft high and I gave her a hand up as the tree bent over like a bow. She balanced. She had ripped jeans on with fishnets underneath and there was a rip across the back pockets with a bit of fishnet covered Neeta hanging out. She had the most gorgeous arse I'd ever seen and it was only about

Damaged Goods

six inches from my face. She laughed, I laughed, Douggie laughed.

'Look Douggie' I said, 'I think you'd better do this. I just can't'... I doubled up with laughter.

We sat back down and had a drink of Red Stripe and smoked a JPS cigarette. We ate the potatoes from the fire and they felt like marshmallows, they tasted grrrreat! Douggie had some torches that he'd made, bits of stick with cloth round the end. We lit them and went to the edge of the grass bank where we stuck them in the ground before climbing up the bank to the top.

It seemed a long way up and when we looked down at the fire it looked hundreds of feet below us, like looking down into a crater. The fire looked like a tiny sparkling, distant jewel and we loved that fire. Look said Douggie, there's more torches! We looked and we saw hundreds of flaming torches amongst the trees. Oh fuck, who's that? Is it villagers come to get us? Have we gone back to the middle ages? No said Douggie, laughing, there's only two really. He was right, we were seeing things, course we were, we were tripping. We laughed and there were only the two little flames down there again. Oh goody!

My head felt like that old gale was blowing through it and we went for a walk through the woods to the edge, leaving the stereo playing. The sand on the paths was glowing! It felt so soft underfoot I could feel it through my cowboy boots. It was beautiful, it was guiding us and making sure we didn't get lost. It was like being in those little dreams that live on the edge of sleep.

We sat at the edge of the woods from where you could see the lights of Milton Keynes and after looking for a while, we decided we didn't like the city anymore. It looked false. It was. Arthur Lee and Love's - 'Sitting on a Hillside' played in my mind. People had been spending money in the pubs and clubs down there and would be feeling rough by now, but we weren't, we felt superior, course we did, we were tripping. We knew the meaning of life. We loved it. Our lives were the same as the trees, like the stars, we were all the same. We felt like we'd come home.

We went back to the fire and It looked so cosy, like it was welcoming us.

The Doors had finished so we put on Nancy & Lee singing 'Some Velvet Morning.' That orchestral backing and their voices sounded achingly beautiful, ethereal. It started to get light as 'Summer Wine' floated out of the stereo and then the music finally ended.

The birds were singing and the first rays of the sun were filtering through the treetops as we walked home. We loved this world, we loved the woods and we loved life. It is the greatest gift. It felt like we'd lived lifetimes in one night. We hadn't even smoked a whole pack of JPS and we'd only drunk six cans of Red Stripe. We felt good and didn't want to go back to the real world. We tidied the fire away and thought wouldn't it be great if everyone could come to a party in the woods...

Well, like most things, it was to start with. We had a few more little gatherings down there as the word spread and the numbers grew, but winter arrived all too soon. Still, Mum and Dad were going away and said it was ok to have a party at their house.

It was a boom time for them, as it was for many in the eighties and Dad had bought himself a big new Mercedes and a lovely new Golf GTi convertible for Mum. They also had a big extension built to the house and bought a place in Lanzarote, which was where they were off to.

So, I went and warned their neighbours and invited everyone I knew, as did my sisters. You expect about half of them to turn up but on the night they all did and there were about 200 people crammed in there. DJ Picci and Gordon bought some of the Camden Palace sound system and set up in the dining room and it sounded fantastic.

Damaged Goods

There were people skinning up on the kitchen table all night, with bags of weed the size of rucksacks and the Scouser had the bathroom mirror down on the table, with mountains of speed on it. Everyone was there and we had one both Friday and Saturday night. The village pub even sold out of takeaways, but not a glass or window was broken all weekend and though there were Stiletto marks in the parquet, from Neeta dancing all night in front of the speakers, the neighbours said they never heard a thing. We said we'd do it down the woods in the summer and everyone said they'd come, cool!

May arrived and finally it was sunny enough for party time down the woods at last. Everyone turned up again, hundreds of them. We met in the village pub and they were in both bars, the beer garden and on the verge opposite, outside Ivan's house. The pub was drunk dry and the landlady asked if I was having a little party and said to tell her next time, so she could order extra drink. We all went off down the woods at closing time and followed the little candles in jars lighting the way.

Everyone was there again, all the Trendies, Soul boys, Bikers, Goths, Punks and Hippies. There were Stilettos in the sand and Fishnets and Farah's mixed in the firelight. At least 100 of them were tripping and so was I. Everyone was having a good time. I'd made these tapes which had Motorhead followed by the Bare Necessities, followed by Divine, The Doors, Donna Summer and the Thunderbirds theme. They made people giggle as they danced in the firelight, with the sparks drifting up to the stars.

We had a few more like that, just before the raves started and they were great, but they just kept on getting bigger. My memories of them are acid dazed now and I think I had probably done too much.

They ended with us moving base to Woburn picnic area, when they finally got too big for the village and I seemed to hardly know anyone who came anymore. People were sawing down trees for firewood and at the last one I went to, someone got shot. What a sad end, who takes a gun to a party? Someone who was scared I guess, but not the sort of person I wanted to mix with, that's for sure.

Still, I don't think they ever found love and peace in 1967 and we sure didn't find it in 1986 - Shame.

Damaged Goods

It was Friday evening and my business for the weekend was done. Douggie called round to say we were going to the Camden Palace, where our DJ friend and Evil Eddie Richards were doing the sounds.

We cruised down the M1 in Douggie's Lotus, tripping, but only half a tab, we didn't want to overdo it in London. The Palace was great and the sounds were brilliant. Vision were singing 'Lucifer's Friend' as we danced the night away and we got some coke, which was nice and clean. My face was numb and so was Douggie's. He said there was something I had to see, so outside and into the Lotus and we were off to The Hippodrome.

It was just before midnight when we arrived and we got in with no problem. The sounds were louder and it was really going some in there. Suddenly it was midnight and it went quiet. Watch this said Douggie, as Wagner's 'The March of the Valkyries' came blasting out. That was some build up. It went dark and suddenly a flying saucer appeared above us in the club. Fuck me! It was spinning and it looked enormous. Oh bloody 'ell! It was only the lightshow. It descended, flashing and spinning above us, suspended from the ceiling and that was definitely something you should see tripping, fuckin amazing! 'Close Encounters' eat your heart out.

We were laughing with a group of girls next to us and they were laughing too. They had big eyes and cut glass English accents and they sounded very posh. They were ballet dancers they said and they were tripping too - great! We talked and laughed some more and got on very well. They told us that they were having a party the next night in Hampstead which was starting at eight and that if we wanted to come, we'd all have a lot of fun.

So, the next night we dressed up in our ripped Jeans, Espadrilles, Baggy Tee shirts, Earrings and Eye liner. My hair was bleached white and Douggies was Jet Black. We took a slow cruise down the M1 to London in my Beach Buggy. When we found the address, we went up the front steps and rang the bell at a big house, with wrought iron balconies.

The girls opened the door and laughed at my car,

'It's great!' they said, 'It's hilarious and cool.'

We laughed too, they were right, it was! We went in and didn't feel out of place at all. The party was full and Simply Red were playing 'Money's Too Tight to Mention.' - Not here it wasn't, this was way cool.

There was Champagne, there was Cocaine and soon enough we were dancing away, talking to everyone. The atmosphere was just great. The atmosphere was verrrry friendly. The atmosphere was 'too rich to care hedonistic.' We even got chatted up by some rich gay guys but just smiled and said no thanks, we were here with the girls. No problem they said.

Somehow, suddenly, it was three in the morning and the party was finally starting to thin out. The girls had their arms round our waists and asked us if we wanted to stay. We laughed and said 'Yes please!' were they kidding!? They had their hair pulled back, wearing diamonds and stilettos and 80's cocktail dresses and they really were beautiful, and fun. They had a gleam in their eyes like everyone had there, which was the coke and we were all giggling as we went up the grand, sweeping staircase.

There were four of them and two of us and we were out numbered. Now ain't that a shame!

The bedroom was bigger than my flat and I had not seen a bigger bed, ever. Honestly. We were all suddenly ripping each other's clothes off, literally and you know when kissing is just like wowwww? Well, it was like that and bloody 'ell, they looked real good with their clothes off.

Terence Trent D'Arby was playing somewhere, coming from hidden speakers and they were indeed ballet dancers. They were supple like you've never seen and they were supple

Damaged Goods

like we'd never seen either and they were very, very naughty indeed, but so were we - what a bleedin' night! Eventually after swimming across them and their silken sheets for hours, it was light outside and we fell asleep.

We all had a late lunch on the balcony, sitting on each other's laps and they said they were off on a tour with the Royal Ballet, but it had been a great night. Yep, it sure was we said. After we all slipped and slid around in the shower together for an hour or so, they waved to us from the door as we drove off and all lifted their nighties and flashed at us. Blimey, Londoners! Now that's a weekend!

Finally I had a bad trip, which was pretty good going considering it had been every weekend for almost 3 years. Like people say – a good one is the best thing in the world and a bad one is the worst. Too right, Jesus!

I thought I'd gone really, totally mad. Flashing through my mind were memories of Pigsy at Glastonbury, of being chased and shot at in the woods by those older guys when I was little, a couple of lifetimes ago. It seemed to be all around me that night, but I guess I just finally caught up with myself and that was enough for me.

I had 12 hours of pure unadulterated fear and ended up sitting under a tree on my own, waiting for the dawn, when I finally managed to think straight enough to remember what dawn was. I knew it should wear off around then and when it did, I thought of everyone else tucked up in bed, safe and warm in their own houses.

What the fuck had I been doing? Three years or more spent partying and now even the speed and coke just seemed to make me feel dirty.

Christ, was that all I could do, escape? Bollocks, I could do better than that. I'd watched everyone else sort themselves out and now it was my turn. It was better late than never and that was my only other choice, which I didn't fancy anymore. I didn't want it tainted by all that I had done and I felt like someone was telling me to stop.

About bleedin' time said Tony when I told him, you should never get high on your own supply. He could talk though, he was importing E's now and selling them to all the Ravers - that's ALL the Ravers. He was making thousands but I wasn't interested in E's, not strong enough for my liking. Like that Bobby Vee song –'Halfway to Paradise.' I really wasn't interested in any of it. I'd got real tired and it didn't seem like fun anymore, just a waste of time, a chemical lie.

I'd started taking stuff to escape and now I felt like it was taking me, stealing my life, present and future.

I guess there's only so many wonderful things to discover in your own mind, and after that, all that's left is shit.

Damaged Goods

Right I thought, no more drugs for me and no more of this lifestyle, let's see how I could do.

I sold my cars like it was symbolic or something, bought a nice, straight and normal Toyota Celica and prepared to reinvent myself again.

What it was, was what it had always been. When I'd left Reading in late 1964 with a new name and a new identity, I wasn't a criminal, I was a six month old baby.

The Beatles were off conquering America, Maria Callas was doing her last comeback concert at the Covent Garden Opera house, Marlene Dietrich was wowing them at Olympia in London, Jacques Brel at the Olympia in Paris, Sam Cooke was slaying them at the Copa, Dr Zhivago was being filmed and I was the little boy who's mummy and daddy didn't want him and gave him away. I was adopted and I know that some people are ok with that, but I wasn't, I was fucked up by it.

I was born Oothur Wilton Brown. My real father was called Arthur and my real mother Jeannette. My adoptive parents had always told me that much, ever since I was little, but that was all I knew. When I went to see them and asked them to tell me anything else they could, they were fine about it, said they always knew that I'd ask one day and they told me plenty.

It seems that I spent the first six weeks of my life in the care of the church in Reading, in a cot in a converted loft, where there were six other cots, all with unwanted babies in.

Fostering was different in those days and though we were all fed and cleaned regularly, we were never picked up, or given any attention, just laid there looking up out of the skylight.

When my adoptive parents came to see me, they were told I was either profoundly deaf, or Autistic, or both.

My adoptive mum was a doctor and loved a medical challenge and took me anyway. She was convinced that I was ok and took me to loads of appointments at Gt. Ormond St Hospital. She gave me my appointment card with my name on it that day, which she had kept.

Finally I had the good fortune to see an Indian doctor, who told them there was nothing really wrong with me, it was just emotional shutdown, which is what babies do if they're

Damaged Goods

left alone, like a survival instinct. I just needed someone to notice me.

I needed to find out why, who did I look like, had they loved me somewhere out there, had they even thought about me, or not?

When I was little, apart from my nightmares, I sometimes had dreams of looking up at the clouds or the stars through a little skylight, with bars around me and. I now knew what they were at last. I still love laying on my back and staring at the sky, even now, I feel like nothing can touch me and nothing really matters and I drift away with the clouds. Shutdown.

As she sat telling me all this, my Mum gave me a moth eaten little green top and shawl and said it was what I came in, the day they picked me up. Bloody 'ell, she'd kept it all those years.

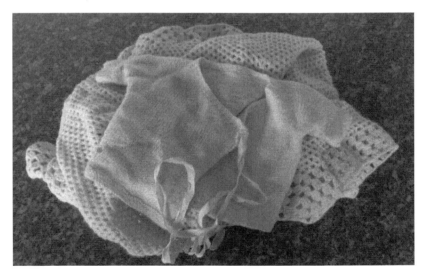

The little knitted clothes that I came in

I thought over what she'd told me and decided that I couldn't put off tracing my natural parents much longer, however it turned out - what if I did and it was too late? I'd have missed the chance to meet them. Hmmm.

I met a girl who worked as a P.A. at my dad's company, where everyone fancied her. She was beautiful and she sort of reminded me of the Scouse girl but she was straight, like I was.

She wore nice clothes and she was so sexy, what a doll. Everyone said no chance but they were wrong. I wanted her and I wanted a normal life. I chose happiness, I chose hard work and I asked her out. She said yes, she said I made her laugh and I guess she thought that would be enough; that and the fact that my Dad was rich.

We went out for two years and I tried real hard, but my attempts at straight work didn't do too well, as it was all new to me. I did all sorts; factory work through a temping agency, delivery driver and even a porter in a piano factory, where I had to sweep up, change the towels in the toilets, unload trucks and everything. I worked for a year selling used cars at a big dealership and had a lot of fun there, getting to wear a suit to work for the first time and bringing home some nice cars on my days off, like A Ford RS Turbo, Renault 5GT Turbo and even a couple of Cosworths.

I sold a lot of cars, but the end of the eighties was also the end of a boom time and when the times got harder, I was the first out the door. I met some good people there though.

We went on a holiday to Mum and Dad's place in Lanzarote with my sister and her friend, where we hired a Suzuki Jeep, to go up to the fire mountains, sat by the pool with cocktails, played cards a lot and dreamed of being rich ourselves. A lot of our friends were.

Eventually though, I guess it wasn't going quite where she expected it to and she finished with me. It hurt but it still felt like unfinished business to me.

She went and lived with an old boyfriend and not long after that, I moved in with an old girlfriend that I'd bumped into. It wasn't right though, just a rebound and neither of us was the same as we'd been before.

Damaged Goods

We did have some good times though. We went to Jim Marshall's birthday party at Cleo Laine's House, getting picked up from our council flat in his chauffeur driven limousine.

All sorts of celebrities were there from the world of entertainment and the charity they ran, The Grand Order of Water Rats, including Julie Rogers & Michael Black from the West End and Mr & Mrs Ernie Wise.

Jim Marshall did a brilliant gig with an all star band, made up from his friends who were present that night. He played the drums for over an hour as he rocked on with Frankie Vaughan, Bert Weedon, Jess Conrad and Joe Brown.

I got to meet them all afterwards, with Frankie Vaughan asking me if I was famous too! What stars that lot are. Also, I have to say that I found Jim Marshall to be a consummate host and a friendly, funny, lovely man.

My Godfather, who'd taken me skiing when I was 12, died and left me a few thousand pounds and after asking my mechanic friend what good cars he knew for sale, I bought a Ford Capri 3.0 S to cheer myself up a bit. It had just been resprayed in metallic blue, with fishnet Recaro's and 2.8i suspension and it was a real babe of a car.

I decided to go and tour round France for a fortnight and do some proper GT driving in it and visit Francis. I did, though we stopped off at Ile de Ré and Chartres for a few nights, before going over to Brive and down to Gers as well. All over really and mostly on the N roads, rather than the autoroutes.

My mint, 3.0s Capri, Ile de Ré, France.

Damaged Goods

We stopped at my Mum and Dad's old friend's place, who used to live in the big house by the forest in England when I was little, for New Year's Eve. They'd got a little Chateau now and it was great and they made us very welcome there, it was a great way to see in a new year.

For the whole 2 weeks the car ran like a dream, cruising all day at 70. On the way back, I got as far as Rennes and stopped at a red light crossroads and watched as a lady in a little Citroen AX came towards me. I was sure she was going to stop but she bloody didn't though and worse, she didn't even look up.

Bang! She smashed right into the front of me. Oh bollocks. I got out to assess the damage and there was a big V in the front of the car, with the bonnet all buckled in. She got out and she had a map in her hand, that's why she wasn't looking up. She told me she wasn't from there, she was from Provence and told me she was on holiday.

'You're on fuckin' holiday!' I said, 'At least you're in the right country… ' But what can you do? We filled out the European accident forms and I tied the bonnet down with my tow rope. The car didn't look such a babe now and I drove back to the ferry slowly.

Back in England, when I got on the M25, this little Nova passed me and there was someone waving, it was Rita. Blimey that's a coincidence, hadn't seen her since the parties in M.K.

Only four years ago, but it seemed a lot longer. I didn't stop but just kept driving, trying to put the past in my rear view mirror.

The girl I was living with didn't work out in the end and after 18 months neither of us was happy really.

One day I got a letter through the door from my ex girlfriend, the girl from my dad's company. Without a second thought I finished with the girl I was living with and moved in with my ex, in her little maisonette.

Sounds heartless now and I guess it was but I was no good at lying and didn't do affairs, couldn't see the point.

I'd got a proper job in the travel industry which sounds good doesn't it? I joined the Railway actually, as a freight guard, which really was starting at the bottom, but at least I was starting and better late than never.

There is nothing romantic about walking around a dark, greasy freight yard in the rain at 2 in the morning, shackling up wagons with a Bardic lamp and I had never worked so hard in my life. I met a lot of good, real people there though and they helped me through it.

There were all those rule books to learn and random drink and drug tests, which I was very pleased to pass, as I had no idea how long stuff stayed in your system, could have been years for all I knew.

Me at old Bletchley station, 1993.

Damaged Goods

I don't think it's so hard to train these days, if you'll excuse the pun, but it was then, trust me. I had to learn things like all the crossover points on the mainline between London and Birmingham, off by heart and it really was down to all of my workmates that I managed it.

Almost like running off to join the circus, it was a life apart, away from everything and everyone I had known, which was the idea. In time I grew to love it and it was like one big family, full of characters. It got me on the straight and narrow, both life and work wise and I have never got off or looked back.

After living together for a year we got married and I was so proud. We had a church do in the village and a great reception, in a big marquee in Mum and Dad's garden. They had sorted themselves out and got back together and all my old friends and family came and we drank and danced the night away to a Disco and my friend's band.

My old friend John gave us a lift to the airport the next day in his Triumph Stag, complete with white ribbon and stuff and for the first time, we flew out to Mum's place in Spain for our honeymoon.

It rained every day though and after spending a week looking out of the window, I finally took the big umbrella from the balcony and persuaded my wife to come for a walk on the beach with me.

We did get to go and see Ronda, Castellar and Puerto Banus, but even the camera that my old friend, Paul the photographer, had given us sprang open and ruined all our pictures.

There was something missing, even then and though I tried to make it good, it wasn't the passionate, loving break that it should have been and was perhaps an omen.

When we got home I was cycling 8 miles a day, getting the train to work and back at all hours and had even started boxing again twice a week. I was fit and was sure that if I just kept working hard, we'd work it all out between us in the end.

Damaged Goods

Tony had finally been busted and did a runner to Spain. He phoned me up and said that he'd wanted to take some time off and travel for a bit anyway, as no one's luck lasted forever. He never came back as it turned out, though not for the reason you might think.

Steve bought a Range Rover Vogue, brand new and very nice, at least I think he bought it, he had a new bike too and I just didn't ask. He'd been doing real well, selling Coke to the rich at Silverstone and at Polo matches and anywhere there was money really, he was like a bloodhound.

I'd kept working hard, taking more exams and progressed to Senior Conductor on passenger trains.

The shifts weren't much better, but at least it wasn't as dirty as being on the freight work and the wages were slightly better too. So we bought a bigger house near her family and mine and I had a normal life at last, or my version of one anyway.

I went with a friend to see the Sex Pistols 20 year reunion concert at Finsbury Park, with Iggy Pop and the Buzzcocks. What a legend, all of them. I gathered that the Pistols didn't used to be so good but they sure were that day, blimey! I was glad they lived up to their reputation, they had always been heroes to me and now they had proved it.

I felt out of place amongst all the punks there, but it also finally felt like my past was a long, long way behind me.

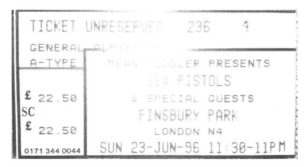

Right, I decided that now was the time and I got in touch with the adoption agency. After a few weeks they contacted me and said that they had a letter for me, from my father, addressed to me. Blimey!

It gave a short message and said he was moving to America. It was 10 years old, but he left his Uncle's address for me. It occurred to me that I must have uncles, aunties and cousins that I had never known. We shared the same blood and might even look like each other. Blimey!

I contacted him and I was so nervous that I told him I was an old friend of my father's from the sixties.

He paused, then said,

'I know who you are. You're his son aren't you? I knew you'd ring one day.'

Bloody hell. I was trying to talk but there was a big lump in my throat.

'You can ring me back when you can talk if you like' he said, but I didn't know if I could go through all that again, so we carried on our conversation.

He asked me my name and. I told him, I swallowed hard, took a deep breath and asked

'Can you tell me about my father?'

'Well, he was studying Philosophy at University when you were born, but gave it all up to be a rock and roll singer' he said.

Blimey, I knew music history, especially the 60's. I put two and two together and it made four.

Click.

I knew who he was talking about, those names on my adoption certificate; it was Crazy Arthur Brown, The God of Hellfire!

Bloody 'ell, Bloody 'ell!

Damaged Goods

I had his 'Fire' LP. Is that why I loved 60's music? Is that why I was the way I was? Blimey.

A few months later he came over to England and I got to meet him at his brother's house, my uncle Colin.

I cried, he cried.

It is very hard to try and put down on paper how that felt and what was said.

Uncle Colin, me and Arthur at our first meeting.

I went with him to visit his mother, my grandmother. I took that little green top and shawl and showed them to her.

'I made those' she said, recognising her own knitting 30 years later.

Oooh how we cried as she said she'd thought of me every birthday and prayed for me. Fuck. I was speechless. What can you say to that?

I also tracked down my real mother, going to visit her a few times.

There was a lot of guilt and anger there for her and it didn't work out too well, you could say.

Doing something like that is like opening Pandora's box, you have to take what you get, but at least I knew who I looked like and I found out that I had old French blue blood in my veins too.

Those 30 years will always be there. I was made by all that and couldn't erase them, but I could forgive though. Life's too short.

Everything I'd ever done seemed to have led to this point and I wished I'd known that there had been one all along.

Damaged Goods

We had a baby, a daughter that we named Lily and she was so beautiful and perfect and innocent but I never felt I deserved her and I think it showed.

I didn't seem to make my wife laugh much anymore, I was working shifts and weekends, doing endless railway exams and I was hardly ever at home. I didn't have time for boxing or anything else much anymore either. She started to love me less and I couldn't blame her really.

This wasn't how it was supposed to be, but I didn't know how to make it right and she didn't either. We were becoming like strangers and couldn't even talk to each other anymore.

When I tried, she didn't want to know, or didn't want to admit we were in trouble and just said

'If you don't like it why don't you leave?'

Ouch. What was I supposed to do? This was the best I could manage for now and it would get better with time, wouldn't it?

I thought we were doing ok. I helped feed my daughter, I changed nappies and I never went out to the pub. I let her spend my money on clothes and I got us a new car, but I was years behind in the getting on stakes.

All her friends had bigger houses and better cars, but they'd all been working hard for years, whilst I'd been partying and she wanted it all now. Maybe I should've stayed drug dealing, I'd be rich by now, maybe you should've she said. Ouch.

I started listening to my Janis Joplin LP's a lot and running through the woods for miles. I needed to see something that wasn't wrong. Why was I dreaming of escape again? Wasn't this what we'd wanted? I guess that neither of us was turning out to be the person we thought we were.

At that time, you were allowed to leave the Railway for 9 months and return to a guaranteed job. I needed more money real bad and couldn't see any further promotion arising anytime soon, so I left and went to work with my old mechanic friend from the next village, who used to have the V8 mini Van.

He had his own business by then and I cycled the 8 miles a day to his garage, which didn't bother me, and tried real hard. He was servicing and tuning cars mostly and I did all that, though it didn't come as naturally to me as it did to him.

We built this monstrous Land Rover, with a racing American V8 engine, mated to an auto Jag gearbox. He got the mating plate for the gearbox from Australia and that thing flew! We had a lot of fun burning off Porsches at traffic lights, though it has to be said that it didn't handle or stop very well!

It was great for a while and I learned a lot, servicing and rebuilding engines and gearboxes, but after 8 months it had become obvious that I was never going to be quick or intuitive enough to earn good money at it myself.

Feeling like I had failed both myself and my mate and was back at square one, I left and went back to the Railway. There were no positions at my old Depot and the only job they could offer me straight away, was at the Willesden Junction Station in London, which meant more travelling, but I took it anyway and got on with it.

Damaged Goods

Big Steve finally got five years for robbery after he was caught putting the last of 12 BMW's onto a transporter at 03:30 am.

Unfortunately the cars weren't his, but he hadn't even broken a window at the dealership he said and it seemed a shame to me, him and his cars.

I went to the court and he just sat there looking bored. When his sentence was handed out he just shrugged, waved at me and smiled.

'See you later son' he shouted. He didn't mind prison, lots of his friends were there, but I was sorry he was going. I felt like the coppers were looking at me too, was I being paranoid? I didn't think so, but in any case it kept me sharp. I just kept on working hard as Mr. Straight.

One day, sitting in the dingy restroom at Willesden, between trains, I saw an advert in the back of the Rail News for a job with Eurostar in London.

Eurostar was the business back then, all new, shiny and prestigious. I sometimes saw the trains passing Willesden, on their way to their new depot at Old Oak Common and thought they looked very flash. The money was good, as was the time off, though the shifts in between were worse and I didn't have any of the qualifications they wanted, but I wanted that job.

I went home and told my wife about it and I could see the pound signs light up in her eyes. I was glad to see anything light up in her eyes to be honest and so my C.V became a work of art. My 4 years of hard work in the industry spoke louder than all the other entries, which was just as well really, as most of them were not much good. By the time I got to the interview, I was so hyped up and enthusiastic that I think it showed and I breezed through it.

A couple of months went by without hearing anything and I'd almost lost hope of getting it, but after we'd been back to Mum's place in Spain again, along with my brother in law and his girlfriend, a letter offering me the job appeared on the doormat. Yes!

There were a few weeks of being measured by a tailor for my new uniform and taking all the medicals, exams and stuff before I started my new job in International Travel with Eurostar as the Fat Controller.

It almost doubled my wages overnight and I was sure that it would make everything better at home.

Me, Eurostar Platform Controller, Waterloo, 1997.

I was so excited that I never even thought about the 3 hours commuting every day, on top of the shifts, but I'd have done anything to make it all right.

Damaged Goods

We had another baby, another beautiful daughter that we named Katya and I thought that things were getting better.

I fawned over her, singing her to sleep, with Janis Joplin's 'Bobby McGee' and Tony Bennett's 'San Francisco,' just like I had with her sister and I was back to feeding and changing nappies. I loved them all so much and I had everything I wanted, except for money.

After a year of hard work and learning the ropes, we went on the train to Paris with some friends and had a single, lovely weekend together. We stayed at a romantic little hotel, up in Montmartre, eating in the best restaurant and sitting outside a bar by the big steps 'til all hours.

Things seemed great there for a change, but when we got back home to reality, my marriage was still going wrong. For all its benefits, work was eating into my home life even more now, such as it was.

One night, just before Christmas, she said I wasn't enough anymore and she was right. I was working my tits off but she didn't do patience. I don't think she believed in me anymore and all of a sudden, I didn't know if I did either.

We'd been together for 10 years on and off and I still didn't know what to do. I still wanted to love her just as much and she was still as beautiful, but that was all we had apart from the kids. Weren't they enough? Work seemed to be the only thing I could get right and maybe I'd just been trying too hard.

I took my Nanny's grandson, Jason, to Paris for a day out and it was his first trip abroad. My brother was doing very well for himself, living in a Penthouse in Battersea at that time and he gave us a load of cash for spending money. We travelled 1st class all the way to Paris, even getting a ride in the driver's cab at 186 mph.

Once we arrived, we saw all the sights and after going up the Eiffel Tower, we spent the afternoon drinking in bars along the Left Bank, just making it back to London to have a final drink with some of my off duty colleagues.

Stumbling down to Euston to get the train home, we decided that we'd probably had enough excitement for one day and didn't bother with the village pub for last orders. That was a good day out.

Damaged Goods

I was listening to a lot of old Cuban music, Mambo, Son, Tango and Caliente, music from another time. Was it any better then? I tried to convince myself that maybe it was. I think that I was trying to get lost in it again and escape.

Arthur got me VIP tickets for The Who at Wembley but she didn't want to go, so I went with my brother and his mates. At the backstage party afterwards I bumped into John Entwistle. The rest of the band was upstairs somewhere in the depths of Wembley and I asked him if he thought Arthur was any good in the sixties. He gave me a surprised look and said 'Yes of course he was, very fucking good' and walked off

I wished I'd met the rest of the band.

Access all areas VIP pass for the Who's 2000 Tour

I got promotion at work, into a different department. I knew I'd been working too hard and I booked us a holiday in Kefalonia, just me and her, no kids.

It was our first proper holiday on our own since they were born and it was a beautiful island, with beautiful weather and a beautiful hotel.

We lounged on deserted beaches, we went on boat trips and we ate out every night, but as usual it wasn't the break I had hoped for.

I tried to talk to her and she just sat there and said 'If you don't like it, why don't you leave?' for the hundredth time.

All that way just to hear that!

We came home to the rain and she finally told me she didn't love me anymore.

She said I was just maybe as good as it gets. I said that everything I had done I'd done for her, didn't she know that? All my hard work? I'd still be a drifter otherwise. She said I had done it for myself.

Christ, was she right?

No, I'd done it for us. But I'd tried to be someone I wasn't and I guess she had too.

Kefalonia, 1999.

Damaged Goods

My days became filled with my thoughts and I wasn't doing too well concentrating on my new job, so I asked my new boss at work for some time off.

I guess as I'd not long been promoted it would have made him look bad and he said no.

I didn't think that was very professional but wasn't in any state to think straight or argue with him. I wished then that I'd never taken the promotion and was still with my old manager, as he would have understood and would have cared about someone other than himself.

Now was the time to be grown up I thought, though I never had seen the point in that and I think my head went then.

Somehow I said goodbye. I don't know how, I was in a daze, I was hurt, but I didn't want to stay for the girls to see their Mummy and Daddy tear each other apart.

When I left I took my clothes, my music and the savings and she got the kids, the house and the car.

I went to stay at my Mum and Dad's for a couple of weeks and though I never expected it, Mum was so kind, talking a lot of sense to me. Then I went to stay at my sister's house, who, along with her husband, was also very kind, but I really wasn't doing too well.

My head went big time and I finally got myself signed off from work after having a bit of a breakdown in the Doctor's Surgery. I had hardly ever been to a Doctor, what with my Mum being one, but when he saw the state I was in, he signed me off work straight away and prescribed anti–depressants and Counselling. Ok, I knew I was in trouble and needed whatever help I could get.

The Who's song from Tommy kept going round in my head, 'Can you see the real me, Doctor, Doctor?' fucked if I could anymore, wasn't sure if there was one. I didn't know what to do. I had to try and keep it together for my girls. I listened to Elvis a lot for comfort, like I did when I was little and I almost wished I still had my little painted cardboard box to hide under.

She never said she loved or missed me, just that she didn't know why I didn't come back. She got someone else, a few months later. I found out when one of my kids told me on the phone and fuck, that hurt.

We got divorced, 7 years plus. I'd known her for 12 and I loved my two children, I still loved her and I missed them all so much. It was torture picking the children up once a week, I couldn't really get my head around it, it just didn't seem to make any sense.

I said a few things to a few friends that I should not have done at that time and they have since forgiven me, but I haven't forgiven myself.

Damaged Goods

I started seeing a French girl that I'd known for a year or two. It was never anything like that, I didn't do affairs. But I didn't do lonely very well either. I'd been signed off work sick and too fuckin' right, I was. Moping around wasn't doing me any good at all and I decided that I had to get away. I went with my new girlfriend to stay at Tony's hotel in Andalucia. He had a house and a hotel over there, as well as a house in Amsterdam and a five bedroom Villa in Goa.

We went horse riding in the mountains, we went to the best restaurants and we drank the best wine. We saw Paco Pena play a Flamenco show in a little backstreet bar in Ronda which was excellent and it all seemed a long way from the UK Decay gigs I used to go to with Tony.

Me, horse riding in Andalucia, 2001.

We hired a Rolls Royce convertible from Marbella Cars, wafting along the road between Ronda and El Burgo, just mountains and olive trees as far as you could see and it was beautiful.

We also had the top floor of a hotel in the old town which was very posh, with a private lift, a roof terrace with three balconies and views across the mountains. We spent money like water and it was great.

Tony said he missed the rain and I said I missed my life. How could it all have been a mistake when my two lovely children came out of it all? The break did me good though, it cleared my head a bit and I threw my tablets away.

Back home and I got a phone call from my mum, to say that my nanny's husband, Derek, had died. I didn't know what to think or say, I had so many memories of him. He'd been more like a Granddad to me, making me my first go kart.

My nanny's husband Derek, in his yard.

I made a speech at his funeral and I don't know how I got the words out really, that was hard. Carrying his coffin with Uncle Malc and Mr Steve gave me a big bruise on my shoulder, like the one I'd got when he taught me how to fire a 12 bore, up in the field behind his house when I was 10.

So, serious rebound. My French girlfriend, who wouldn't? She was beautiful, she was a dancer and a singer in the theatre. She'd got divorced and said her ex husband had been a coke dealer in London. It never occurred to me then that he might not have been the bad one.

Her family lived in Marseille. They owned a casino, nightclubs and bars. They owned an island and high-speed boats. They wore gold rings on their little fingers and they had machine guns in their houses.

We got a flat together in Kensington, which was ok, though we sometimes heard funny noises from the neighbours. She did shows in London, she did shows in Paris and we went all over, even my Mum and my daughters came up to see her. She was great.

At work I got a fortnight off every eight weeks and we went on lots of holidays, all of us going to stay with her parents and we did the Conde Nast guide of hotels & restaurants together.

One evening I got back to the flat and as I walked into the shared hallway I saw our neighbours. Two gay guys, Giovanni and Eric, both naked, well, almost. Giovanni was on all fours, wearing a pair of Donkey's ears and a tail, making donkey noises. Eric was chasing him down the hall singing opera and when they saw me, they froze. Oooh sorry, they said, I smiled and told them not to let me spoil their fun.

They went into their flat and shut the door and I went into mine and I guessed that explained the funny noises we heard! I put on my Amanda Lear LP, she was singing 'Give a Bit of Mmm To Me,' 70's Camp Disco at its best. I turned it up as I thought they might appreciate it, but I could still hear Eric singing his opera at the top of his voice and Giovanni braying, but at least it was muffled now. I was glad to see that Londoners hadn't changed and started to feel better.

A couple of nights later, me and my girlfriend were sitting out on our terrace drinking Mojito's we'd made with the mint from our little front garden, when Giovanni and Eric came down the steps. They apologised again for the other night and I laughed and offered them a drink. We all sat outside together drinking and smoking until the sun came up, having a great time getting completely hammered.

We went to Strasbourg for a long weekend and rented a lovely big apartment in the old town, which was all beamed houses and little canals.

We took a boat trip to look around for the afternoon and ended up eating at a very posh restaurant called La Tannerie, where we had Choucroute cooked in Champagne. It was served by a waiter in white gloves which was very expensive, but you can't disguise Choucroute - it was still just a pile of cabbage with bits of meat sticking out of it. We ended up at a hotel bar that was done out like Club Tropicana from the 80's, drinking cocktails 'til the early hours, finally stumbling onto a tram to go home.

The following morning we took a day trip over the river to Germany and toured around the Black Forest in a chauffeur driven car. I could speak fluent French but German was totally alien to me, I didn't even know how to ask where the toilet was. We visited the Casino at Baden Baden, where her family knew someone and we were treated like kings, even getting a horse drawn carriage for the day to take us around the sights. Nice.

Chariot for the day, Baden Baden.

We went to stay with Tony again too. He had a bar and a restaurant on the Costa now. He was looking at another hotel and he spoiled us. I had a suntan in winter and we bought endless clothes and we hardly ever ate in. Somehow it didn't feel right to be enjoying myself though.

A month or so later, we went out to stay with her family again and went out in the bay on their boat, swimming and playing around, with Elvis and Tony Bennett playing on the stereo and it felt real good to be in the sun.

Me and the Med!

Damaged Goods

I was back to work and after getting the Union involved, my new boss had back pedalled, or been told to, and I was given back my old job, with my old mates and my old manager, bless him. I was real glad to be back, though I don't think that place ever felt the same again to me.

Over the years I got to meet loads of stars at work, like The Bee Gees, Jimmy Cliff, Aerosmith, Oasis, Johnny Depp, Michael Palin, Monica Belluci and Honor Blackman. They were all friendly, lovely people, but there were exceptions.

I was there late one evening and after a train had arrived from Paris, I heard someone shouting outside my office. I walked out onto the platform and there was one of my assistants, arguing with David Soul, from Starsky and Hutch! Blimey!

It was over the unlit cigarette in David Soul's mouth and the assistant was being a real pain in the arse. I told him to go away and tried to placate my childhood hero, who was that night, quite rightly, a very pissed off six foot cowboy. I told him that when I was little I wanted to grow up to look like him and have a car like Starsky.

He just looked me up and down and said 'guess it didn't work out huh?' and walked off.

Well, I tried!

There was another time when I bumped into Liza Minnelli with her new husband, just getting off a train. I told her that I loved her music and her husband asked, with a sneer, what my favourite song of hers was. Quick as a flash, I replied 'The Sound of Your Name,' recorded live in Paris with Charles Aznavour.'

That shut him up and Liza just smiled at me and gave me a peck on the cheek. Ha ha ha.

I met Kylie Minogue a few times too, when she was travelling to Paris and I got a signed book and photograph that she wrote dedications to the girls in. They thought it was great and it was too, Kylie was such a babe.

Kylie's book, that she signed for my girls.

I got a signed book from Paul Weller as well, though that was just for me.

Damaged Goods

We used to have a lot of fun at that place sometimes, getting control to make 'double entendres' announcements over the PA system, for people like 'Dr Seymour Beaver' and 'Mike Hunt' and even hopping on the trains when the train managers weren't looking, making cringe worthily camp announcements to all the passengers for them.

We also used to give ourselves silly call signs to use over our own walkie-talkies, like 'Sugar Pants to Fluffykins' and broadcast things like 'I've got a big one slipping in behind me' when a train arrived.

We tried to see how far we could go without using bad language really and usually got away with it.

Practical jokes were often the order of the day and there aren't many places that could reduce you to tears of laughter at 05:30 in the morning, but that place was an exception in many ways back then and our team was a great bunch of guys and girls, like its own little family really.

I don't know how our manager put up with us sometimes and he must have fielded a lot of complaints on our behalf. What a guy.

We did do a lot of hard work too though, consistently beating both Paris and Brussels in the monthly right time departure contests.

The Control hut, Waterloo International.

We bought a little house in Hertfordshire, where we always ate out and had wild parties with mountains of Cava. Even Giovanni and Eric came down from London to my daughter's birthday party once and they seemed to get on well with her theatre crowd.

We played Charles Aznavour, we played Les Negresses Vertes and we played The Gipsy Kings.

Her family came to stay, sometimes all of them and sometimes it almost seemed like she didn't want me to like them, but she had her reasons for being in England I guess.

'Look after our little girl' they said and I said I'd try.

We went to stay with Tony in Spain again and this time he didn't look so good. He spoilt us rotten though, taking us to his friend's restaurant where he even chose the wine. Blimey, him a wine buff? Things sure had changed all round.

Two years earlier, Tony had a little altercation with the locals, Jose and his band of Gypsies. He thought Tony was there to smuggle and sell drugs on their territory, but he wasn't. This was a place to hide for him, that was all. They threatened to cut his throat when they came down and broke all the windows in Tony's bar.

The next night he went and burned out one of their caravans and pushed one of their cars over a cliff and it kinda stopped after that, until a month before. They had turned up at Tony's place during the town Fiesta, drunk and rowdy, so Tony had barred them and they'd stood outside and shot out his windows again. Oh dear.

So anyway, there I was, 2 years later, back in Spain, sitting there with my girlfriend and in walked Jose and Co. We'd seen them earlier on that day in the street, when we were stood talking to Tony and they'd given us a real nasty look, before walking off.

They saw me and started staring at me, talking to each other and pointing over at us. Oh shit, it suddenly started to feel like the good the bad and the ugly. I could die here I

Damaged Goods

thought and I was only there on holiday, it wasn't even my problem!

I told my girlfriend not to move, took a deep breath and went up to them at the bar. I bought them all a drink and Jose gave me a real hard stare and it was one of those moments that could have gone either way.

I told him that Tony didn't want to muscle in on his smuggling and did not want a war. I held my breath as he stared at me some more.

I knew they were probably armed and that I was not, I was on holiday! What a fuckin' idiot.

Suddenly though, he clapped me on the back and laughed. OK he said and told me I had 'grandes cajones' - big balls! He said sometime perhaps we should talk some more, but not now though, tonight he said, lets drink. So we did and after a few more, they finally left.

I went and sat back down and about 10 minutes later, Tony walked in. That was lucky, it could have got very messy.

I didn't know about having big balls as I'd been terrified really, but I guess it looked good. There were different rules up there and the Federales never came out at night, people were left to sort their own problems out mostly, like we had. It was a long way from home.

The next night, we took some wine and drove up into the mountains, stopping at the roadside up near Capilleira, parking in the scrub. It was the annual night of the shooting stars again and I got the feeling that a lot of things were turning full circle.

After walking for 10 minutes we reached an old Shepherd's casa. There were some of Tony's friends already there, who'd ridden up on horses earlier to get a fire going and it looked like I'd finally found the wild west

We sat there watching the light show and the stars were much brighter than in England, it was lovely. They were all smoking Morroccan dope, I couldn't stand that stuff anymore, though I still liked the smell.

We talked all night and I was glad I was amongst friends. If you follow people like that into the middle of nowhere at night, either you're friends or you don't come out and I guessed that I wouldn't have been the first.

As dawn approached Tony's friends rode off into the sunrise. Shouldn't that have been sunset I wondered?

The clearing near Capilleira, Spain.

Tony turned to me and said,

'Remember this.'

What?

'Remember this won't you?'

'Course I will' I said.

He gave me a long stare and put his arm around me.

'Great innit?' he said.

Yep. But I felt a chill run through me, like someone had just walked over my grave.

Damaged Goods

'Ok,' he said finally and pulled a ring out of his pocket. Said he'd bought it for me in Thailand. Platinum with a blue Sapphire from Burma, like the sea he said. I thought it was a ladies ring but I wasn't gonna say.

What was Tony doing buying me jewellery? Strange night.

Then home to grey skies and England. Turned out my natural father, Arthur, knew my favourite 60's band 'Love.' How cool was that?

We got tickets to see them perform the 'Forever Changes' album at the Royal Festival Hall. What a beautiful gig.

Afterwards we went backstage and met my heroes. They were all so friendly and signed everything for me. Wow.

Arthur Lee and me, backstage at Guilfest, 2003.

I met loads of people through Arthur, including Tim Rose of 'Hey Joe' fame. What a guy he was. He did a tour with Arthur and we went to St. Albans with a load from the village. It was an excellent gig.

I got to meet Arthur's other son too, he'd come over from America with him for the tour. He was a Martial Arts expert, but seemed very gentle and it was great to meet a brother that I never knew I had.

Damaged Goods

Tim Rose spoke to me like a kind old uncle and we had endless phone conversations, where filled me in on the 60's. Saw him at Blackheath Halls too, where he dedicated a song to me. Oh my, Oh my.

Tim Rose and me.

A month or so later, we went to see Joaquin Cortez at the Royal Albert Hall doing his Flamenco show and that man sure can dance. Best of our generation they say. Too right, he was stunning.

Arthur was on tour with Motorhead and Hawkwind and we went to see them at Wembley, where he got us VIP passes. Wow.

I got a great photo of them all onstage doing 'Silver Machine.' My girlfriend kept walking on stage whilst they're playing and I thought it was funny, though the bouncers didn't.

Me, Lemmy and Arthur, backstage at Wembley.

After the gig we went to the backstage party and it was how you might imagine backstage at a Motorhead and Hawkwind gig should be, wild! We ended up drinking brandy at a hotel near Luton airport at 4 in the morning. Blimey.

It was a bit of a social whirl you might say for a while. Arthur was playing Guildford Festival, along with Love, The Darkness, Alice Cooper and Billy Bragg amongst others. He got us VIP passes again and I got to meet them all too. How cool is that.

Damaged Goods

I got a phone call from Steve. He was out and going to buy a house on the Costa. See you there son he said, no more England for me. Why don't you come out here with your family? I told him I was divorced now.

'Fuck I'm sorry son' he said.

A few months after he'd gone, I heard a few rumours about people getting shot and disappearing over there. I wondered for a while, but kept any thoughts to myself, probably best.

Tony phoned and said he was off to Goa as Senor Incognito.

My girlfriend got cancer. We got her the best treatment we could and made endless trips to Hôpital Saint Louis in Paris on Eurostar, at least we travelled free.

Finally the cancer went, just a little scar healing up. Her head wasn't though. She went a bit crazy. She got jealous, she got violent and she started going off with other men, then phoning me afterwards to tell me about it.

Despite all her punches, kicks and biting, I never hit her back, it wasn't my style. I loved her but she just got worse. One day I came home to find her crying, sitting in a cold bath with a kitchen knife. It was hurting her and it was killing me. I just wanted it to be right. Which one of us was crazier?

I started worrying about waking up with a knife in my neck, which didn't seem beyond the realms of possibility and worried for my daughters too. It all ended, as badly as it could. Stormy weather was here again.

She moved back to France to her family and luckily they understood. That was the only good thing from it. I sold the house and sent her half. I left everything that we'd bought in it. The dishwasher, the freezer, the washing machine, the sofa, the glass top table and chairs, even the bed. All that lovely oak flooring that my neighbour had helped me put down too. Ah well, fuck it.

All I took was my clothes, my books and records. My head went again and I was feeling very sorry for myself. I moved back to my parent's house in the village at 39 years old, how sad is that? I was starting to think that I just wasn't cut out to live on the straight and narrow.

Then things really went crazy. My ex wife phoned to tell me that she'd heard Punky Suzy had died from an overdose in London, on the game. That made seven of my friends dead in three years and all under 40, but not me. Why not?

Oh fuck. Another phone call from Arthur to say that Tim Rose had died in hospital, never coming round from the anaesthetic he'd had for a 'little operation' that he'd mentioned, when I'd spoken to him 3 days earlier and arranged for him to come round for a meal.

Oh Fuck. The next thing was Steve phoning me up, to tell me that Tony had died in Goa, just like that and there hadn't even been an autopsy or a body, as the Indians had burned it and put it in the Ganges, apparently.

I had already booked my flight to go and see him, but I wouldn't be going now though, or ever again.

I made a speech at his memorial service but I cried a bit and fluffed it. It wasn't just Tony, it was all of them.

I hummed Elvis to myself and wore the ring he'd bought me.

Steve was there. There were people from Leighton and Spon from Luton. They cried.

There were people from The Costa as well who shouldn't have been in England, this wasn't supposed to happen.

We were all supposed to be living happily in the sun by now, not that we'd ever actually said it, but 20 years was gone, just like that.

Damaged Goods

Me and Tony's money was in a Luxembourg bank and I couldn't get it without our joint signatures and they'd probably start asking all sorts of questions now anyway, so it was as good as gone. Fuck the money. I was tired of it all.

I went home and lay there listening to Frank Sinatra singing 'In The Wee Small Hours of the Morning,' trying to drift back in time and be somewhere else.

I started going in the village pub a lot where I grew up. It sort of felt like home and was the nearest I had.

I was back to where I started from, without a pot to piss in. I was in the worst mess of my life and felt like the walking wounded.

Still, I had some old friends there and I soon made some new ones. They didn't know the other me and I tried not to think about it.

The Landlord was a friend of mine. He loved Elvis too and he played some good stuff in that pub, Green Day, The Pixies and The White Stripes 'Elephant.' It was a welcome distraction. I hadn't been listening to much modern stuff for ages. What happened to me? I'd always loved music. I guess I got sidetracked.

I started going horse riding through the woods and went to watch the Polo matches at the stables down the road and generally tried to relax a bit.

Joey and me, Stockgrove Park.

Me and the landlord went to see The Brian Setzer Big Band in London. I had liked him when he was in The Stray Cats, but wasn't expecting too much to be honest. Just shows how wrong you can be. What a guitar hero that man is.

By the end of the gig he was sliding across the stage on his knees, big quiff, bare chested with his jail house tattoos and doing these amazing guitar solo's, as his band blasted out behind him and the crowd going wild. Brilliant night!

I had three weeks off work and went to Australia, it was as far as I could get. I flew with Air Malaysia and was very well looked after, stopping off in the palm covered Kuala Lumpur en route. I realised how big Australia was when we reached the coast and it still took almost another 5 hours to reach Sydney.

I stayed with my brother, who lived there now and had a nice place on Manly Beach. He came and met me on his way to work at 06:30 and gave me his keys, so I took the ferry around the bay and found his place without too much trouble. Before I went to sleep, I sat out on his balcony with

Damaged Goods

a Tooey's beer, watching the parrots fly by, looking at the sea and it felt very foreign.

We went out to a party that night and ended up playing pool with a couple of off duty hookers in Kings cross. They were good fun and afterwards we walked back through Kings Cross to get a cab without any trouble at all, driving back across the harbour bridge at 4 in the morning. He had got some good friends out there and it was good to see him.

Sydney Harbour, Australia.

I took a bus out to Spit Bridge and walked back, around the coves of Sydney Harbour National Park. There were jungle plants and noises out there and I saw a load of big Golden Orb Spiders, in a web stretched right across the path. When I rounded the end of a cove to see Pink Flamingos standing on the beach, I realised how far I was from England.

I went on the train up to the Blue Mountains for a few days on my own, which was worth it just to see the scenery as it rushed past. Just as well as when I got there, it was too misty to see the views, so I went and saw them on a big screen indoors instead. I took a tourist bus for a few hours after that and ended up staying in a Walton's type house hotel in Katoomba. It was lovely, right at the end of the road and when I walked back there after a night in the friendly bars of Katoomba, it was so dark beyond the last streetlight, that the world just seemed to end.

The next morning I was woken by an Australian magpie singing outside my window at 6 am. They don't look or sound like English ones and when I went out on the veranda and sat in a chair, it hopped over and sat right next to me and it all seemed kind of surreal, like a giant film set. Great country and great people, what a beautiful place.

My holiday was over, I'd got my head straight and I went back to England. I just went to work, saw my girls on my days off and hit the pub at night time, otherwise I didn't seem to sleep too good. I grew my hair and bleached it, why not?

A couple of months later, I took the girls to Mallorca for a week. It was the last of my money from the sale of the house, so at least something good came from it all. There were just the three of us and we booked all inclusive. The hotel was only three star and a long way from what I'd been used to, but it was good anyway, near the beach and most importantly for the girls, it had a lovely big swimming pool.

So our days were filled with Ice Cream, food, swimming pool and more Ice Cream, sometimes we did beach, swimming pool, Ice Cream.

We took a boat trip in a glass bottomed boat, that we had almost to ourselves. The skipper steered us in and out of caves, as the Beatles hits played on his stereo.

Damaged Goods

Katya and Lily, Porto Cristo, Mallorca

Another day we went over the road down into a big cave, to watch as some rowing boats drifted across the massive underground lake, carrying a small orchestra who played some lovely classical music.

In the evenings they had all sorts of competitions and I won the big one on the last night, where I had to do all sorts of silly things, much to the girl's amusement.

I think that was the best holiday that I ever had. The girls were so good it made me happy and sad, as I saw what I was really missing. Still, the holiday was over and home we went.

I came off a quad bike whilst burning around in my Mum's fields and I got a broken shoulder, broken collarbone, a few cracked ribs and a hole in my hip where the broken brake lever stabbed me.

I was out cold for about an hour and came round with a nasty bruise already appearing all round the back of my head. The rest of me was covered in cuts, grazes and more bruising which turned some lovely colours, what a state. Me, Ozzy Osbourne and Rik Mayall - Some club!

I somehow got up and drove myself to the hospital, but once I'd been cleaned up and it all started hurting, there was no way I could drive back and I had to leave the car there and get a lift home.

Now I was as bruised and broken as I felt on the inside. Perhaps it was some sort of message not to take everything for granted and concentrate on living.

I got some pain killers which were good, as the NHS did good gear, and I was in a bit of a daze for a while too, which helped.

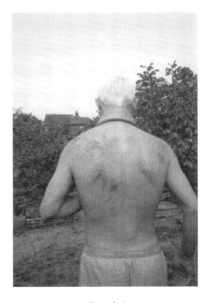

Ouch!

Damaged Goods

I was signed off work for 3 months even sending them a photo of my injuries, in case my mates thought I was pulling a fast one, when my boss came all the way to visit me.

I wasn't too ill to limp along to the pub with my arm in a sling though and I did so most nights. Not a lot else I could do though to be honest.

After 2 months of hanging around, I was getting bored and started walking in the woods, trying to get a bit fit. I'd only got about a mile when I fell over a tree root and with a loud crack, tore the ligaments in my ankle.

'Well, Fuck my luck' I thought and almost laughed – That was a first for a while.

Finally I went back to work again and was glad to see that nothing much had changed. It gave me a sense of normality, somewhere to belong, somewhere I could get things right and find friends that didn't keep dying.

Sunrise from my old place, Linslade.

I was 40 by then and into extra time and I was trying. I was living in a rented 2 up 2 down, tucked away in the old part of town, hidden off the road through an arch in a conservation area and nice and quiet. It had a lovely private little courtyard garden round the back, from where I could look out over the rooftops and see the church tower all lit up at night. Made me think of Bordeaux.

It belonged to some friends from the village and was in a right state. It needed revamping, a bit like me, but they let me have it cheap. People can be very kind.

I painted it from top to bottom and to be honest, it gave me something to concentrate on.

Luckily, I had an old friend who was a builder. He put in a new kitchen and bathroom for me and it started to look like a proper little palace. Anyway, I kinda liked living somewhere where you could hear the wind blow and the gutters overflowed when it rained, it felt real.

I was lost in music. I had a mountain of CD's and Vinyl and I played it all. I couldn't find any answers in there anymore though.

It had been like the soundtrack to my life and maybe I should stop listening to it all now. But I didn't have anything else and what should I do, sit in silence?

I was listening to old stuff like Little Richard, The Beatles, Joan Baez, Neil Diamond and Sweet, Slade and T Rex, my records from when I was little, when things were simple.

Still trying to borrow emotions from the songs I guess. Maybe if I listened enough I could start me again, with a clean slate and maybe even if I didn't I could be a real person, instead of me.

Did that make me a fake? Does it matter? Like Gloria Gaynor sang 'I am what I am'.......

I drank too much and I smoked too much. The Eagles sang that 'Some drink to remember, Some drink to forget' but I was just drinking, to a new future and I'd keep going until it arrived.

Damaged Goods

My Shoulder and collarbone got better, as well as my ankle and I started running through the woods again, ten miles sometimes. I kinda wanted to just keep going for ever and would have probably given it a try if it wasn't for my kids.

Arthur was in The Darkness's video for their hit 'Is It Just Me?' and I got to go and be an extra, all dressed up, in the London church where it was filmed.

We had a lot of fun and all went and had Christmas dinner together in a hospitality trailer, somewhere under the Westway, very rock and roll!

That was a fun day out and what friendly people they all were.

Justin Hawkins and me, Christmas 2006

I went on the Eurostar to Paris and then took the TGV down to Bordeaux to stay for a weekend with Francis. We had a lovely time and as usual him and his girlfriend Bea spoilt me rotten. Why didn't I ever notice what a lovely city that is?

We drove up through the vineyards to St. Emilion for lunch, stopping off to pick up cases of wine that Francis had ordered the year before. Life went on. Sitting out in his garden, eating supper with his friends, we had wine, Cognac, Cigars and Eau de Vie and I felt safe there.

Francis, me, Max and Bea, Bordeaux.

It wasn't like at home, where I always felt like a stranger, I didn't mind feeling like a stranger when I was abroad. It was like a different world that I had a VIP pass to visit and I felt very lucky.

You know what? I liked France. It wasn't tainted like Spain was for me. The Atlantic washed everything clean each night, unlike the Med and they had Joie de vivre and a slower pace of life and that's what I wanted.

Damaged Goods

Finally I was starting to feel honest. I was still here.

My children are the best thing I've ever had. They are the best thing anyone ever has. I wish I'd known that all along, but I was trying to be a good dad, in absentia. I made them laugh a lot and I saw them every week.

Their mum's fella was rich, they had a big extension built on the house, bought a Porsche and they got married. She was happy.

I missed my ex wife, the way it was and I missed my ex girlfriend, the way it wasn't. I missed Tony and I missed Steve.

I seemed to have a long list of people I missed. The further back I looked, the more there were.

It had been my choice, once upon a time, but I never even realised it.

I missed out on a normal life. I'm starting to think that maybe I should have done it all for the money after all, it sure would be handy now, yes indeedy.

I'd been richer. Owned nicer places to live and had some flash cars, but you know what? I'm still a walking cliché - Money never made me happy.

I was trying to forget my past. That's why I have written it down, to get rid of it from inside my head.

There were many times when no one thought less of me than I did and I'm still trying to invent a better person. I still have enough time to make it right and I want it.

My old mechanic friend was doing real well and had his own Race Team. He'd started out with TVR's and moved on from there.

He took me with him across France, to drive down and buy some Dodge Vipers a couple of times because I spoke French, but also because we were still good friends and enjoyed each other's company.

Me in the all conquering, Viper GT.

I always had a brilliant time with him, looking round all the factories and race tracks, sitting in the cars and wearing a shirt emblazoned with his team logo. He even flew me and his brother out to Lyon once, to look at a Maserati for a weekend and the other team treated us like kings.

He is a wise old owl, my mechanic friend and one of the most gifted people I have ever met.

Along with Douggie and others, he talked a lot of sense to me many times when I was in a mess and I am grateful to have such good friends as them.

When my first book was published, he had the title and publishers name sign written on the back of his cars for me as a surprise. That was some good publicity!

He even got me VIP passes so I could take my Nanny for a day out at Silverstone. She is the world's No1 Race fan and loved walking round the pits and into all the team garages, talking with the drivers and especially standing up on the firewall as all the cars raced by.

My nanny, Mrs S, at Silverstone.

I even started to play guitar again, for the first time since punk days. I could hardly play a note anymore really, but I enjoyed it.

No rock for me though, I was learning Flamenco, like when I was little and still dreaming of Spain, with a copy of Laurie Lee's 'When I Walked Out One Summer's Morning' sitting on my bedside table.

I was listening to Loretta Lynn's album, - 'Van Lear Rose', with Jack White, it's a great album and Iris Dement's LP, 'Lifeline.' 'God Walks the Dark Hills, to Show Me the Way.' Well, I wasn't sure about that, but someone sure did. It's hauntingly beautiful. Country Rock and Mountain Gospel? Blimey. Hey - It was good enough for Elvis.

Amy Winehouse's album, 'Back to Black' was just out then too and what an album that is, like The Ronettes on gin. I played it nonstop for a while.

I also listened to Cesaria Evora and Mariza's Fado music, sung in Portuguese Creole, or Tom Waits' dark, mysterious poetry, the fabulous Pink Martini and even Donna Summer and her Disco fantasyland, which was probably the one big party that I missed out on.

I'd put it on when I went to bed and drift away.

One thing I knew was that I was good at surviving and I also knew when something was over. I finally felt almost happy.

It was like leaving home at 16 with nothing again, except of course I was 40 and divorced with two kids. You've got to laugh really.

I took up Salsa dancing and I loved it. Me and my little girls danced in the front room. I had to buy Tony Christie's 'Amarillo' for them and we'd all sing along in the car and the front room. I could remember it on Radio 1 the first time around, a lifetime ago, and suddenly it seemed to have gone so fast.

Damaged Goods

I must have been getting old after all. Never expected to and never had a plan for it.

UK Decay got back together and I went to see them at their comeback gig. It was brilliant to see Spon and all my old punk friends again and they played just as well as ever.

They have been headlining Punk and Goth festivals all round Europe ever since, and their singer, Abbo, recently married Cerys Matthews, the singer from Catatonia.

Me and my old friend Steve Spon, from UK Decay,

Me and my old friend Mattie went to the launch party for Arthur's latest album 'Vampire Suite,' which was the best album he'd done for years. It was held at his old friend Simon Drake's House of Magic in London, and was a proper rock party.

There were loads of famous people there, including another of Arthur's old friends, Lena Lovich, who is just the same in real life, as in her act, fantastic!

Arthur and Lena Lovich at Simon Drake's House of Magic.

Simon did his whole magic act up on stage, culminating in very realistically chopping off Arthur's head and then talking to it and it was another great night.

Damaged Goods

Spain is a country of many contradictions. The locals on the over developed Costa genuinely smile at the people who buy their land, with words and numbers on a piece of paper and imagine they have really bought a mountain. But you only have to go inland a few miles, to find tiny whitewashed villages, seemingly lost in time and a peace that is only disturbed by the wind.

One afternoon in July, when I was next there, I went for a walk up in the hills by myself and followed a stream, which ended in a waterfall. I stripped off at the water's edge and swam in a pool deeper than me. That's all the escape I need these days.

The next day found me sitting on my friend's boat in 39 degrees, 10 miles off the coast of Marbella, eating breakfast. The sea was smooth as glass and warm like a bath. I even managed to water ski earlier and we saw dolphins and pilot whales on the way out.

You see even then I wasn't without friends. I was lucky and I wasn't done with Spain either, I still liked it there and life sure could have been worse.

Playtime on the Costa del Crime!

I started more horse riding lessons too, with Ivan, 30 years since my last one. He was 60 by then and I could ride ok, but there's riding and then there's riding.

My girls had lessons and were soon better than me. They wanted to come riding with me in the mountains and I said we would, but maybe not Spain though.

I am lucky. They are my little angels and I finally found my reason for being here, which is the best one in the world and shouldn't have been a surprise really.

I took my little girls to see Joaquin Cortez at the Albert Hall again which was just as good as the first time I saw him.

A few weeks later I took Lily to a gig by Arthur Lee and Love. What a lovely bunch of guys and what a gig. We went backstage to see the band afterwards and they were all great with Lily.

Lily and Johnny Echols backstage.

Damaged Goods

I had a few girlfriends in the five years that I lived at that little place, though it never seemed to work out, but I wasn't really surprised. Maybe I'd just go it alone for a while, that'd be novel and probably best.

It bears reading; it didn't bear living, not really. There were a lot of good times and I tried to remember them. Mostly though, I tried to forget.

I've always been an outsider and it wasn't a pose, I was born like it and I reckon I'll die like it too. Not just yet though, I'm not finished.

There's a song on Don Maclean's American Pie LP, 'Crossroads' and the Lyric kept going round in my head. Sort of all roads lead to Rome thing which seemed apt.

I'd like to have been cool and said Edith Piaf's 'Non, je ne regrette rien' instead, but that wouldn't be true, as I did, plenty.

In 2005, Arthur had a career retrospective at The Astoria in London. I went along with some of my old friends, including Pigsy and had a whale of a time. He did three separate gigs over the course of the night, showcasing his three incarnations, as The Crazy World of Arthur Brown, Kingdom Come and lastly his more recent solo stuff. It was a brilliant night, with all the old stage props, including Kingdom Come's giant crucifix, which he was attached to.

The whole show was compered by his old friend, Howard Marks, also known as Mr Nice, who I got to meet, amongst others and found to be a wonderful, witty and warm raconteur.

I wasn't to see Howard again until Glastonbury 2011, where he recognised me straight away. Just shows that there is nothing wrong with his memory, in spite of what we are led to believe! He has also read my book and likes it!

Me and Howard Marks, aka Mr Nice.

Damaged Goods

In 2010 it was the 40th anniversary of Glastonbury. Arthur had played at the very first one and was again booked to play. He got me and my girlfriend Amanda VIP passes for the whole weekend and we camped out in the staff camping area. We got to use the backstage bars, restaurants and even their toilets, which was nice!

My 2010 Glastonbury Artist's pass.

Arthur did a great set with his band and also sang a storming version of his hit 'Fire!' with Johnny Clark, Jerry Dammers and his Spatial AKA, up on the main pyramid stage.

We wandered round the site all weekend, bumping into my old friends, The Mutoid Waste Company and their weird sculptures and vehicles and saw loads of singers and bands, from all era's.

The highlight for me was to see my all time favourite band, the legendary Funkadelic, now that was a show!

Afterwards, we got to go to the backstage party, where we drank and mingled with all the stars and even got to stay up late!

Me and Suggs, backstage at Glasto, 2010.

Me and Jerry Dammers, Glasto, 2010.

Damaged Goods

What else? I speak fluent French and passable Spanish, though none of the schools I went to taught me. Life is the best teacher I have found, it's just a case of being able to hold on and ride the bumps.

When I read this and look back, I think I see 25 years of stupid, but then sometimes I don't think too good. What can I tell you? I was born blond! The little boy who's mummy and daddy didn't want him and gave him away.

I think I was the price of fame and I think I was lucky to get out of it.

I would have been the son of the King of the Hippies, The God of Hellfire. Guess that would have made me the Prince of Darkness and maybe I spent my life trying to run away from it.

He sang 'I Put a Spell on You' and I've got that tattooed on my shoulder in French - Ensorcelé. Someone's sure been looking after me and I guess a spell would've done it.

So, there you have it. Quite what anyone reading all this will think of me I really don't know. I never did anything bad out of malice, though sometimes I made bad choices and did bad things out of stupidity, or for good reasons, like fun, love and loyalty, but what else is there?

Anyway, the past finally seems a long way away and there is a future in front of me. Like Mr. Wilde I may have been in the gutter, but I'm looking up at the stars.

I have found that love and peace can be elusive things and I am trying to live the sort of life where I might find them now.

Glass half full and I ain't finished yet.

That's it!

P.S.

I worked on the Railway for 17 years, almost 13 of them spent with Eurostar. For a long time, it was the best job in the world. It allowed me to go backwards and forwards to France for free, many times, but eventually, after all those years of working shifts and weekends, the glitter wore off. When they offered voluntary redundancy in 2009, I took it, along with my girlfriend Amanda from their management team, much to their surprise.

In the 2 years since, I have successfully studied to gain qualifications as a Practitioner of NLP, TimeLine Therapy™ and Hypnosis.

Doing those things was the catalyst that allowed me to finish this book, enabling me to write the final chapters and close my past, once and for all.

We now live together in a house in my old village, which has a lovely view over the woods and valley, where all those parties were, some 25 years ago and we are looking forward to our future.

Damaged Goods

My adventures into the world of Rock n' Roll continue. I went to Glastonbury 2011, as road crew with Arthur and had a whale of a time, getting to watch from backstage many performers and eating and drinking with even more of my musical heroes. Here's a couple of photo's from what was a great weekend.

Nik Turner, the Hawkwind legend and me.

Me and the wonderful Linda Lewis

As an official roadie, apart from the cleaner toilets, cheaper less crowded backstage bars and restaurants, where I could hobknob to my heart's content, I had to lugg costumes and prop cases around and blagg our car through the crowds to park right next to the stage with a security escort, when we didn't have the right pass.I am very grateful to all the lovely security people we met, who made our weekend so hassle free.

One of my other duties though, was to light Arthur's Fire helmet,that he wears when he sings his song Fire! In the event, in spite of what seemed a dangerous amount of lighter fluid, I couldn't get it to light and had to hold the lighter right on it, burning my hands. I guess it isn't everyone who's done that and certainly not everyone has burned their hands setting fire to their dad's helmet...!

Damaged Goods

If you want to see more info and pic's, you can have a look on my Facebook page;

 http://facebook.com/damagedgoodsbook

 For more info on Arthur, you can have a look at the biography written by Polly Marshall, 'The God of Hellfire,' or his fansite, http://www.arthurbrownmusic.com

And last but not least, for the latest on UKDecay, you can find them on http://www.ukdecay.co.uk

Copyright ©J. Wolfendale 2011

Printed in Great Britain
by Amazon.co.uk, Ltd.,
Marston Gate.